PRACTICAL
GOURMET

Company's
Coming
®

Celebrating
150 Years of
Canadian Cuisine

Jennifer Ogle
James Darcy

Library and Archives Canada Cataloguing in Publication
Ogle, Jennifer, 1972-, author
        Celebrating 150 years of Canadian cuisine / Jennifer Ogle,
James Darcy.

Includes index.
ISBN 978-1-988133-46-1 (softcover)

        1. Cooking, Canadian. I. Darcy, James, author II. Title.

TX715.6.O452078 2017   641.5971   C2017-900728-9

Cover credits: *Front cover:* Nanaimo bars: NoirChocolate/Thinkstock; Maple syrup:
creighton359/Thinkstock; Pastry: Photography Firm/Thinkstock; Wood texture: MiroNovak/
Thinkstock; Maple leaves: chaluk/Thinkstock; Smoked salmon bagel: martinrlee/Thinkstock;
Fiddle heads: bhofack2/Thinkstock. *Back cover:* Fall leaves: AlexRaths/Thinkstock; Tourtiere:
martiapunts/Thinkstock; Poutine: Fudio/Thinkstock; Hawaiian pizza: 12875116/Thinkstock.
All other cover photos are by Merle Prosofsky.

All inside photos are by Merle Prosofsky and Nanette Samol except: p. 4 (Design Pics),
p. 5 (Hemera Technologies), p. 6 (mirceax), p. 7 (Design Pics), pp. 44–45 (HandmadePictures),
pp. 74–75 (LauriPatterson), pp. 118–119 (Elena Elisseeva) and pp. 134–135 (tapui), courtesy
Thinkstock.

Distributed by
Canada Book Distributors - Booklogic
11414-119 Street
Edmonton. Alberta, Canada T5G 2X6
Tel: 1-800-661-9017

We acknowledge the financial support of the Government of Canada.

Funded by the Government of Canada
Financé par le gouvernement du Canada | Canadä

PC: 28

CONTENTS

Introduction

In this book I have chosen not to celebrate any one culture; I celebrate all the cultures that have come to Canada. We do not have enough room here to do justice to them all, but I hope this might be a joyful homage to some of the many flavours of Canada that we have embraced as our own.

The celebration of the cultural mosaic of Canada was given a focus of multicultural diversity during the years of Pierre Elliott Trudeau. He described Canada as a "mixed stew" rather than the "melting pot" expressed in the United States' ideal of assimilation and cultural conversion. We are all separate and unique chunks of the stew, distinguishable, but we are all in the same pot. Joe Clark later took that a step farther when he said that "Canada has a cuisine of cuisine. Not a stew pot, but a smorgasbord."

I live in the epicentre of Gastown in Vancouver. Just two blocks away from me is an example of the epitome of Canadian cuisine. This is where the Chinese smorgasbord was first created in 1870. As the Chinese began arriving in British Columbia following the Fraser River Gold Rush of 1858, they created a community just near Maple Tree Square. Scandinavian loggers would ferry across the harbour from the North Shore. The Chinese cooks would set up tables made of slabs of wood with benches for the buffet of dishes. They didn't need to speak each other's language; they could just point or fill their own plates.

So our cuisine is a buffet of our cultural heritage, but we put it on the same plate and it mixes and merges and mingles. I just had dinner with my friend who was born in Taiwan, raised in Japan, trained in classic French cuisine and is now the executive chef of a well-known Italian restaurant. All of these cultures shape his understanding and appreciation of food. Canadians are like that. We embrace our own history and each other's diverse cultural heritage—especially the food.

Canada's oldest cuisine comes from our First Nations. Filtered through the various cultural lenses of waves of immigrants, the native ingredients still form a fundamental base of the traditional cuisine. Maple syrup, smoked salmon, bison jerky, fiddleheads, wild berries and mushrooms, oysters and clams all have their place in an Indigenous diet many thousands of years old. In the memory of our land we find traces of the cuisine that came before us.

My *Kokum* (grandmother) was Metis and Cree. She would treat us to cooking the wild—to fermented plants, moose and bison broth and frothy Indian ice cream. She would add any number of elements from other cultures, using her staple of available ingredients as the base. And she was always so excited to taste something new. She told me about her first orange: she shared it with her family and friends, pinching the vibrant rind for days before they ate it together, cherishing every bite. We are fortunate to enjoy each other's cultural cuisines. Through the simple act of sharing we can celebrate both our heritage and our differences.

Perhaps the first great European-Canadian cuisine was developed by the early cod fishing fleets that arrived even before the official discovery of the land we call Canada. By 1580, 10,000 fishermen made the voyage each year to harvest our cod, drying or salting it for the return trip to sustain a needy Europe that required non-perishable meat to eat on the holy days that made up over half of the year. Herring could not survive long, and the eel from the ponds of northern Europe was plentiful but not as tasty.

When Samuel de Champlain crossed the Bay of Fundy in 1606 to Port Royal from the first colony at Isle St Croix, he created our first culinary society: *L'ordre du bon temp*, or the Order of Good Cheer. Most years, my friends and I celebrate this mid-winter event commemorating Champlain's attempt to bring happiness and health to his settlement after their first year of starvation and death while stranded on the island. We serve venison and quail with frozen wild berries and mussels smoked atop pine needles, a dish that was well known in Champlain's home region of France. When the British took the settlement in the siege of Port Royal in 1710, they were treated to a *chaudier*e of shellfish by the French cooks. They took this dish with them to the other colonies of New England, and it became their New England clam chowder.

Many Canadian dishes originated with our French, British and Aboriginal ancestors. In many cases it was a mixture of these peoples. Bannock, originally called *pakwejigan* when made from corn mixed with the wheat of a Scottish pan bread, is now served at every powwow, universally adopted as an Aboriginal staple. The Gaspe region of Quebec is famous for its salmon cipaille, which may have come from the early meat sea pies of the British. Most Quebec hearths early on would hold a smoked *jambon* (ham) that was later modified *aux cabane a sucre*, drawn from the native traditions of tapping the maple sap in spring.

The waves of immigrants arriving in Canada were largely supervised by the French and British governments as opposed to the slightly more random settlement in the United States. Large numbers of immigrants from the same countries settled on adjacent land in Canada and reinforced the shared community of their culture. Many communities built communal ovens to bake the breads of their homeland and gathered to celebrate their traditional feast days with food, beverage, song and dance.

The eastern Europeans perfected the unique brining of Montreal Smoked meat. And the Montreal bagel is of course unique from others of the world. Jewish settlers brought some of these traditions west. German peoples brought farming and fermenting traditions that still survive. Ukrainian pioneers brought perogies and cabbage rolls. There are Dukabour communities in BC, Mennonites in Ontario and Manitoba, Japanese in Vancouver and an Icelandic community in Gimley, Manitoba.

These groups and others did not always have their traditional ingredients. Chinese vegetable dishes grew to include available broccoli and onions. The Hungarian colony in Fort Qu'Appelle, Saskatchewan adapted their goulash to the bison and peppers they had available. Breads from all over the world often kept their unique shapes and recipes but were changed by the new strains of wheat that we developed in Canada. Pastas and pizzas took on new forms as they adapted to the different properties of these new varieties.

There was also the sheer inventiveness of Canadians who created new dishes with new ingredients. The Yukon Gold potato, the MacIntosh apple and Red Fife wheat changed many dishes. Ginger beef was invented by George Wong of the Silver Inn of Calgary. And Tojo of Vancouver invented the BC roll and the inside-out Tojo-maki that would later become the California roll. Hawaiian pizza was invented by a Greek in Edmonton, Alberta or in Chatham, Ontario, depending on which side of the pizza war you support.

Canada is a luxurious buffet of culture and unique flavours that remind us of who we are and how we came to share this country. We may all have a recipe that we think most exemplifies the mixed stew of Canada. I will claim my favourite as the warm bowl of Metis Rubaboo stew that my grandmother would serve us as kids. I hope you have one such dish in your own family. May you find other traditions and tastes in these pages.

Habitant Pea and Butternut Squash Soup

Serves 4 to 6

Most countries have their own version of traditional pea soup, which isn't surprising given that peas have been cultivated since the very early days of civilization. When legumes reached France in the 800s, they soon became a staple food for European peasants. Later, in the 1600s, peas were brought along on the explorations of New France, which would extend from Newfoundland to Lake Superior and from Hudson Bay to the Gulf of Mexico by 1712. French Canadian pea soup was created by these early settlers, who were called *habitants*. The *habitants* began to grow peas as their primary crop to survive after disastrous wheat crops during the early 1800s. Later, Habitant became the brand name of a much-loved canned version of the soup. The following recipe is a modern interpretation using butternut squash and different spices.

1 Tbsp (15 mL) oil, such as canola or sunflower

1 large yellow onion, diced

1 Tbsp (15 mL) minced ginger

1 tsp (5 mL) toasted and ground cumin seeds (see Tip)

2 star anise, whole

4 bay leaves

2 tsp (10 mL) turmeric

4 cups (1 L) water

1 cup (250 mL) split yellow peas

6 cups (1.5 L) unsalted vegetable stock

1 medium butternut squash (2–2 1/2 lbs [1–1.2 kg]), peeled and diced

2 Tbsp (30 mL) maple syrup

sea salt and fresh pepper to taste

fresh chives and plain yogurt to garnish (optional)

Heat oil in a heavy-bottomed pot. Add onion, ginger, cumin and star anise and cook until onion just begins to caramelize, about 5 minutes. Add bay leaves, turmeric, water and peas and simmer, uncovered, until peas are tender, about 40 minutes. If peas become dry, add some stock. Add squash and any remaining stock. Cook until squash is tender and cooked but still holds its shape, about 15 minutes. Remove and discard star anise and bay leaves. Stir in maple syrup and season with salt and pepper. Pour into individual bowls, and garnish with a swirl of yogurt and fresh chive spears, if desired.

Tip

To toast cumin seeds, heat a small pan over medium-high heat. Add seeds and toast, stirring, for 1 to 2 minutes or until very fragrant but not smoking. Remove to a small bowl immediately to stop cooking,

You can serve the soup as it is or purée it for a smoother, creamier soup.

Habitant Pea Soup (Québec Pea Soup)

Bring water and split peas to a boil over high heat. Reduce heat, add bay leaves and simmer until peas are tender, about 1 hour. Meanwhile, sauté onion in butter until translucent. Add celery and sauté for 5 minutes. Once peas are ready, add stock, onion mixture, carrot and ham to pot and season with salt and pepper. Heat soup through and discard bay leaves. Serve with crusty bread and butter.

**Habitant Pea Soup
(Québec Pea Soup)**

4 cups (1 L) water

2 cups (500 mL) split yellow peas

4 bay leaves

1 large onion, diced

1/4 cup (60 mL) butter

1 cup (250 mL) diced celery

4 cups (1 L) hot vegetable or chicken stock

2 cups (500 mL) grated carrot

2 cups (500 mL) diced, smoked ham

sea salt and fresh pepper to taste

Maudite and French Onion Soup

Serves 4 to 6

The oldest recorded evidence of soup dates back to 6000 BC—the soup was made with hippopotamus. The word "soup" comes from the English "sop," which comes from the Old French, *sope* or *soupe*. Bread was a vital part of soup (unlike today where soup is soup regardless of bread) because it was used in lieu of a spoon. Soup was more often than not simply the liquid or drippings from cooking, which were poured onto bread to sop them up. Working with recipes brought from France, French Canadians have developed a reputation for wonderful French onion soup. Traditional French onion soup, unlike the kind with heavy beef stock that most people are familiar with, is a simple soup made only with onions and simple seasonings. Older versions of French onion soup do not have cheese broiled on top; this addition dates from the early 1900s.

1/2 cup (125 mL) unsalted butter

1 Tbsp (15 mL) sunflower oil

5 medium onions, thinly sliced (a mixture of types works well)

sea salt and freshly ground pepper

1 Tbsp (15 mL) balsamic vinegar

1/4 cup (60 mL) minced garlic

1 bottle Maudite beer (341 mL)

4 cups (1 L) vegetable or chicken stock

3 sprigs fresh thyme

2 bay leaves

1 tsp (5 mL) Dijon mustard

splash of sherry

6–8 slices of sourdough bread, toasted

Gruyère cheese, grated

Melt butter and oil in a heavy-bottomed pot over medium-high heat and add onions. Season with salt and pepper and cook until soft, about 10 minutes. Add balsamic vinegar, turn heat down to medium and cook onions for 45 minutes to an hour until dark and nicely caramelized. Add garlic and sauté 5 minutes. Add beer and simmer until it starts to reduce, then add stock, thyme, bay leaves and mustard. Bring just to a boil, then simmer for about 20 minutes before adding sherry and adjusting seasonings. Ladle hot soup into ovenproof bowls, top with the bread and cheese and broil until golden brown and bubbly.

With a name that means "the damned one," La Maudite is from the famous Québec microbrewer Unibroue and contains 8% alcohol. Over the past decade, many micro- and artesian brewers have emerged throughout Canada, offering superior, small-batch beers to connoisseurs. Canadians spend over 6.7 billion dollars per year on beer, accounting for more than 51% of the sales of all alcohol combined.

Sweet Corn Bisque

Serves 6

Corn, often called maize, is believed to have been developed from a native grass in Mexico over 7000 years ago. It grows well in rough soil and is far more reliable than crops such as wheat. Corn was vital to early Native peoples throughout the Americas. They made porridge and unleavened breads such as johnnycake, ate corn on the cob and even enjoyed popcorn. Introduced to corn prior to 1000 BC, First Nations living near the Great Lakes and the St. Lawrence learned to grow it and began to trade it for skins and meat. When he visited Hochelaga (now the site of Montréal) in 1535, Jacques Cartier found widespread cornfields, and Samuel de Champlain found the crop under cultivation near Georgian Bay 80 years later. Corn was also instrumental to the survival of the first explorers and settlers. It became important to the fur trade when intermediaries such as the Algonquins traded corn for pelts from more distant tribes.

8 cups (2 L) corn kernels, fresh from the cob or frozen; reserve 2 cups (500 mL) for garnish

1/4 cup (60 mL) butter, plus 1 Tbsp (15 mL)

sea salt and freshly ground pepper to taste

2 cups (500 mL) chopped yellow onion

1 clove garlic, minced

3 stalks celery, diced

2 medium carrots, diced

2 sprigs fresh thyme, minced

6 cups (1.5 L) stock

1 cup (250 mL) heavy cream (32%)

Tabasco to taste

tarragon sprigs and thinly sliced red pepper for garnish

In a pot, sauté reserved corn in 1 Tbsp (15 mL) of butter until cooked, about 5 minutes. Season with salt and pepper and set aside. In same pot, sauté onion in 1/4 cup (60 mL) of butter until translucent. Add garlic, celery and carrots and sauté for 5 minutes. Add remaining corn and thyme, cover with stock and simmer for 20 minutes. Purée in batches in blender to make a smooth soup and return to heat. Stir in cream, and season with salt, pepper and Tabasco. Garnish each bowl with reserved corn, tarragon and red pepper. Serve hot.

Corn Bread

Preheat oven to 400° F (200° C). Sift together flour, baking powder and salt. Stir in cornmeal. In a separate bowl, cream butter and sugar together, then beat in eggs, one at a time. Stir in buttermilk, then lightly fold wet and dry mixtures together, being sure not to over mix. Bake in a 2 buttered 1-pound (1 L) loaf pans for 30 to 35 minutes or until tester comes out clean.

Tip
For a great Canadian version of this corn bread, use maple sugar for the sugar.

Corn Bread

2 cups (500 mL) flour

1 Tbsp (15 mL) baking powder

1 tsp (5 mL) sea salt

2 cups (500 mL) cornmeal

1 1/4 cups (310 mL) butter

1/3 cup (75 mL) sugar

3 eggs

2 cups (500 mL) buttermilk

Borscht with Fresh Lemon and Dill

Serves 6

There are so many varieties of this wonderful beet soup in Central and Eastern Europe that it is hard to find where the first borscht was made. Beets were originally cultivated for their leaves, which were eaten much like spinach; it wasn't until the early Christian era that the roots became popular fare. Ukraine became the major grower of beets in Eastern Europe. In Ukraine, borscht is taken very seriously as the national soup, and Ukrainians firmly believe it originated there. Encouraged by offers of free land, as many as 170,000 Ukrainians immigrated to Canada in the decades following the 1890s. They largely chose to settle together in the wooded parkland regions of the Prairies that were reminiscent of their homeland, and here they maintained their culinary traditions. Today, foods such as borscht, pierogi and cabbage rolls are popular across the country.

3 Tbsp (45 mL) butter

2 medium onions, diced

sea salt and fresh pepper

2 stalks celery, diced

2 carrots, diced

2 parsnips, diced

2 cups (500mL) shredded cabbage

4 cloves garlic, minced

3 medium potatoes, diced

5 medium to large beets, (1 1/4–1 1/2 lbs [575–750 g]), oven roasted, cooled and grated

6 cups (1.5 L) chicken or vegetable stock

4 cloves allspice

juice of 2 lemons

1/4 cup (60 mL) fresh chopped dill

sour cream and additional dill for garnish

In a large pot, melt butter and add onions, season with salt and pepper and cook until onions begin to turn golden. Add celery, carrots, parsnips, cabbage and garlic, and sauté for 5 to 7 minutes. Add potatoes, beets, stock and allspice, bring to a boil, and then immediately reduce heat. Simmer, uncovered, until potatoes are tender, about 15 minutes. Add lemon juice, dill and salt and pepper to taste. Serve in individual bowls and garnish with sour cream and dill.

Roast Beets

Roasting beets in the oven concentrates their natural sugar and produces great flavour. You could also use this method (without the baking sheet) on the barbecue.

Preheat oven to 400 to 450° F (200 to 230° C). Scrub beets well and place on a large piece of foil on a baking sheet. Rub each beet with olive oil and season well with salt and pepper. Add a few sprigs of fresh thyme and a bay leaf. Scrunch foil around beets to contain liquids. Bake beets until tender, about 45 minutes. Set aside until cool enough to handle and slip skins off. Use in adjoining recipe or serve on their own, sliced, diced or grated—hot or cold—with a dressing, blue cheese and walnuts or a bit of butter or sour cream.

Wild Mushroom Soup with Parsley Froth

Serves 6

Foraging for mushrooms is a pleasant, if somewhat closely guarded, pastime for many Canadians, and a good selection of fine edible mushrooms is to be had. Morels, chanterelles, lobster and pine mushrooms are the finest selections for both commercial and home foragers, and they all dry well for winter storage. Wild mushrooms can be found from coast to coast, but the bulk of commercially harvested wild mushrooms come from British Columbia. The pine mushroom in particular is known to have been traditionally eaten by the Nlaka'pamux (Thompson River) and Stl'atl'imx (Lillooet) peoples of B.C. Farther east, Iroquois people enjoyed several types of wild mushrooms, including morels and giant puffballs. The year 1871 brought Canadians the first published mushroom field guide, *The Mushrooms of Canada*. In the early 20th century, Japanese immigrants began to collect the pine mushroom for consumption and for sale. Today, B.C.'s multi-million-dollar wild-mushroom industry ships to Japan and Europe as well as the U.S. and domestically.

3 cups (750 mL) fresh, cleaned wild mushrooms, such as chanterelles, lobster or morels

2 Tbsp (30 mL) olive oil

1/4 cup (60 mL) unsalted butter

1 large yellow onion, diced

2 large Yukon Gold potatoes, diced

1/4 cup (60 mL) dry sherry

1 bouquet garni of parsley, thyme and bay leaf

3 dried juniper berries, bruised

4 cloves garlic, minced

8 cups (2 L) chicken or vegetable stock

1 cup (250 mL) heavy cream (32%)

Slice mushrooms into even-sized pieces and sauté in batches in a large pot with olive oil and half of butter until nicely browned. Remove mushrooms and set aside. In same pot, melt remaining butter and add onion and potatoes. Sauté until golden, then deglaze with sherry. Add bouquet garni, juniper berries, garlic, sautéed mushrooms and stock. Bring to a boil, then immediately reduce heat to a simmer and cook until liquid has reduced by one-third. Add cream, bring almost to a boil and remove from heat. Remove bouquet garni. Purée soup in a blender until smooth. Serve hot, garnished with parsley froth (see opposite).

Parsley Froth

Blanch parsley, drain and squeeze dry. Purée parsley and pass through a fine mesh strainer. Scald milk in a pot, remove from heat and add parsley. Just before serving, blend with an immersion (stick) blender until frothy.

Parsley Froth

1 cup (250 mL) fresh parsley, chopped

1 cup (250 mL) milk

Warning

Because some mushrooms contain deadly toxins, eat only mushrooms positively identified as edible.

Tip

If suitable fresh wild mushrooms are not available, you can use half the quantity of dried wild mushrooms. Reconstitute them in hot water or stock for about 10 minutes. Add enough liquid to cover, using a small plate to keep them submerged. Save the liquid to add to your soup; it will be full of great mushroom flavour.

Clam Chowder and Tea-smoked Scallops

Serves 6

An east coast favourite, chowder as we know it today is a thick, creamy soup frequently but not always made with seafood, as well as potatoes, onions and celery. The word "chowder" comes from the French *chaudière*, meaning "cauldron" or "kettle." In the fishing villages of 16th-century Brittany, fishermen would contribute part of their day's catch to a community stock pot. Villagers added vegetables, hard-baked biscuits and whatever else was handy, such as butter or cream, with everyone getting a share of the *chaudière*. The practice came to Newfoundland with Breton cod fishermen, and from there it spread to the Maritimes. Following the British seige of Port Royal in 1710 and the subsequent Acadian expulsion from the Maritimes, the recipe spread south to New England. There are many variations of clam chowder. The recipe below uses scallops instead of the traditional salt pork, a food staple on sailing ships in the olden days.

Clams

2 cups (500 mL) white wine

2 cloves garlic, minced

sea salt and fresh pepper

4 lbs (2 kg) hard-shelled clams, well scrubbed

Scallops

2 Tbsp (30 mL) sugar

2 Tbsp (30 mL) rice

1/4 cup (60 mL) oolong loose tea

6 Digby scallops, shucked

olive oil for brushing scallops

In a large pot, bring wine and garlic to a boil, season lightly with salt and pepper, add clams and cook until they open, about 5 minutes. Discard any that do not open. Transfer remaining clams to a bowl. Reserve liquid (clam nectar), straining with a fine mesh colander.

Line a wide pot with foil (to save your pot and make clean up a snap). Sprinkle sugar, rice and tea on foil. Brush both sides of scallops lightly with oil. Place a wire rack, such as a small cooling rack, in pot and position scallops on rack so that they do not touch. Turn heat to high. When tea starts to smoke, cover pot tightly and reduce heat to low. Cook for 4 to 5 minutes. Turn off heat and let scallops rest an additional 2 to 3 minutes.

In a heavy pot, sauté onions in butter and oil until golden. Add vegetables, bay leaf and reserved clam nectar, and cover with stock. Simmer for 15 minutes, then add clams and cream. Simmer for 10 to 15 minutes more or until potatoes are cooked and soup is reduced and creamy. Ladle soup into individual bowls, and garnish each with a scallop and sprinkle of herbs.

To make your chowder more "Acadian," sprinkle dulse, a powdered seaweed product available in health food stores, into each bowl.

Tip

For best results, time the scallops and chowder to be ready at the same time.

You can substitute 1/2 cup (125 mL) diced bacon, cooked until crispy, for the scallops. You could also dice the scallops and stir them into the soup, or use smaller bay scallops.

For the chowder:

2 medium onions, diced

1/4 cup (60 mL) unsalted butter

1 Tbsp (15 mL) olive oil

2 cups (500 mL) diced celery

1 cup (250 mL) diced carrots

3 medium potatoes, peeled and diced

1 bay leaf

reserved clam nectar

fish or clam stock, enough to just cover vegetables

clams, as prepared opposite

2 cups (500 mL) heavy cream (32%)

scallops, as prepared opposite

1/4 cup (60 mL) fresh herbs, such as parsley, thyme or tarragon

Bison Carpaccio Salad

Serves 4 to 6

Bison were extremely important to the Natives of the Prairies, providing everything from nourishment and clothes to medicine. Raw meat and organs from a freshly killed bison were a delicacy, and it was considered an honour for the hunter to consume them. The Métis created elaborate traditions around the hunt, and bison played an important part in their culture as well. An essential survival resource for the Métis, the bison also provided goods for trade, most notably pemmican. Until the late 1800s, there were between 30 and 70 million bison on the North America prairies. Within just a few short years, the pressures of settlement, agriculture, drought and sport hunting had driven the bison almost to extinction, thus threatening the existence of an entire way of life. Many years of hard work and dedication have saved the wild bison population in Canada, and today we can enjoy this highly nutritious and great-tasting meat from farm-raised herds.

1 clove garlic, minced

2 shallots, finely diced

1/4 cup (60 mL) extra virgin olive oil, plus additional for drizzling

1 Tbsp (15 mL) balsamic vinegar

1 lb (500 g) bison tenderloin

sea salt to taste

3 Tbsp (45 mL) freshly crushed peppercorns

2 Tbsp (30 mL) grainy Dijon mustard

1/4 cup (60 mL) chopped fresh parsley

1/4 cup (60 mL) chopped fresh dill

baby salad greens, washed and spun dry (about 2 cups [500 mL]) per person

1 bunch fresh radishes, sliced

fresh chives, thinly sliced

Combine garlic, shallots, oil and balsamic vinegar in a bowl. Place tenderloin in a pan and coat evenly with garlic mixture. Let marinate in fridge for 4 to 6 hours.

Remove tenderloin from fridge and pat dry. Season well with sea salt and peppercorns, and sear over high heat (or grill) until nicely brown, about 5 minutes. Remove from heat and let cool.

Rub mustard over entire surface of tenderloin and then roll in fresh herbs. Wrap tightly in cellophane and freeze for 3 hours to make slicing much easier.

Slice meat as thinly as possible and serve with simple greens, radishes, fresh chives, a drizzle of olive oil and a sprinkle of sea salt.

Tip

Be sure to allow yourself the 4 to 6 hours needed for the marinating and a further 3 hours for freezing. You can prepare the carpaccio ahead of time by slicing the tenderloin and laying the slices out in a circular pattern in a single layer on individual serving sized plates, covering well with cellophane and keeping in the freezer up to 5 days. Because the meat is so thinly sliced, it thaws within 5 to 10 minutes. Don't leave it longer than that because, when left too long, it loses its nice red colour.

This dish is named after Renaissance artist Vittore Carpaccio, whose work often displayed a predilection for red. Carpaccio is most often made using beef, but many foods work well in the style of carpaccio. Ultra-fresh tuna, salmon and other seafood make excellent carpaccio; just garnish with your favourite citrus. Vegetables such as zucchini—or even apple and other fruits—work well garnished with shaved cheese and toasted or candied nuts.

Heirloom Tomato Salad

Serves 4

Introduced to Canada at the end of the 18th century, the tomato was slow to catch on until it was found superior to mushrooms and fermented fish in a condiment called ketchup. Tomatoes are now a country-wide favourite, but Leamington, Ontario, is the Tomato Capital of Canada. With the highest concentration of greenhouses in Canada, Leamington was also home to the Heinz ketchup factory and produced most of the country's ketchup for over a century. Although the factory is no more, the tomatoes remain. If you are interested in tomatoes reminiscent of days in the garden as a child picking the sun-warmed fruit right off the vine, seek out heirloom varieties.

1 clove garlic, minced

splash of white balsamic vinegar

1/4 cup (60 mL) olive oil

sea salt and freshly ground pepper to taste

1 lb (500 g) heirloom tomatoes, washed, cored and sliced ½ in (1 cm) thick

1/2 lb (250 g) bocconcini, sliced the same thickness as the tomatoes

handful of fresh basil leaves, washed and patted dry

French baguette

In a salad bowl, add the garlic, vinegar and oil. Then add the tomatoes, tossing gently to coat with dressing. Season to taste with salt and pepper.

On individual plates, layer tomato slices with bocconcini and some basil tucked in between and around the tomato slices. Scatter remaining basil leaves on top and drizzle with remaining dressing.

Serve with slices of crusty French baguette.

Tip
Fresh tomatoes from the garden or the farmers' market would also work in this recipe.

Bocconcini is a semi-ripe mozzarella cheese that comes in small, soft, white balls.

In her tomato book, the late Lois Hole, beloved lieutenant-governor of Alberta and long-time gardening guru, wrote about the importance of heirloom varieties in maintaining gene pool diversity. Lois called this contribution priceless because heirloom seeds are used in developing new varieties that have natural resistance to viral, fungal and bacterial diseases.

Minted Coleslaw

Serves 8

Often regarded as a health food, cabbage has been cultivated since before recorded history, although at first it was merely a few leaves and no head. Pythagoras recommended cabbage for longevity, and he lived to be over 80. He especially liked cabbage raw with vinegar, similar to Montréal-style coleslaw. Rich in vitamin C, which protects against scurvy, cabbage was an important crop for the pioneers, both fresh and, more importantly, preserved, as in sauerkraut. Jacques Cartier has been attributed the honour of planting the first cabbage in New France during his third voyage, in 1542. The word "coleslaw" comes from the medieval Dutch *kool sla,* meaning "cabbage salad." Seeking to augment rural populations following World War II, the Canadian government wooed immigrants from the Netherlands, which had a surplus of farmers. Approximately 185,000 of these "preferred" immigrants arrived on our shores between 1947 and 1970, settling largely in Ontario, Québec, Alberta, Manitoba and B.C. Today, coleslaw graces nearly every Canadian picnic and barbecue.

2 Tbsp (30 mL) grainy Dijon mustard

2 Tbsp (30 mL) sour cream

1 Tbsp (15 mL) mayonnaise

1 Tbsp (15 mL) olive oil

2 Tbsp (30 mL) apple cider vinegar

1 head Savoy cabbage, shredded

1 small head purple cabbage, shredded (about 2 cups [500 mL])

1 fennel bulb, shredded

1 carrot, grated

6 radishes, grated

1/2 cup (125 mL) sliced green onion

1/2 cup (125 mL) fresh mint, thinly sliced

Whisk together first 5 ingredients for dressing. Toss vegetables together in a large bowl and add dressing. Toss well and let marinate at least 30 minutes.

Tip

You can easily turn this recipe into an Asian slaw by omitting sour cream, mayonnaise, olive oil and mint and substituting 1 Tbsp (15 mL) toasted sesame oil, 1 Tbsp (15 mL) soy sauce and a handful of toasted sesame seeds. Grilled and sliced turkey or chicken breast also make a nice addition.

Montréal-style Coleslaw

Using mostly vinegar and only a touch of oil, this refreshing salad is sure to make your mouth pucker. It goes well with grilled and roasted meats. For best flavour, make a day ahead.

Toss vegetables and salt together, place in a colander and let sit for 30 minutes. Squeeze any excess moisture out of vegetables and toss with remaining ingredients. Cover and chill overnight. Toss again before serving. Serves 6.

Montréal-style Coleslaw

1 large green cabbage, thinly sliced

3 carrots, grated

1 bunch green onions, sliced

3 Tbsp (45 mL) flaked kosher salt

3 Tbsp (45 mL) unbleached sugar

2/3 cup (150 mL) white wine or champagne vinegar

3 Tbsp (45 mL) olive oil

Smoked Salmon with Asparagus Salad

Serves 4

This incredibly delicious salad offers the opportunity to use many amazing B.C. products, including fresh asparagus, cranberries, honey and, most importantly, smoked salmon! This delicacy of the West Coast is generally on the top of the list of items visitors like to take back home with them. This recipe uses cold smoked salmon, or lox, as it is sometimes called, which is salmon that is cured but not cooked, so it has a unique flavour and texture. Smoked salmon is available as hot smoked, jerky, Indian candy or even as Tandoori nuggets. Be sure to try one of these products the next time you are at your local fish counter.

1/4 cup (60 mL) dried sweetened cranberries, coarsely chopped

1 Tbsp (15 mL) capers, drained and chopped

2 tsp (10 mL) honey

2 tsp (10 mL) balsamic vinegar

1 garlic clove, minced

2 Tbsp (30 mL) olive oil

sea salt and freshly ground pepper

1 x 2 lbs (1 kg) bunch of asparagus, trimmed

5 oz (150 g) cold smoked salmon slices

1/3 cup (75 mL) crème fraîche (see Tip)

1 large, ripe avocado, sliced

chives and dill for garnish

Combine cranberries, capers, honey, vinegar, garlic, oil and salt and pepper in a small saucepan. Stir over medium heat until warm. Let stand for 15 minutes to allow the cranberries to soften.

Blanch asparagus in a large saucepan of boiling, salted water for about 2 minutes or until bright green; drain. Immediately place asparagus in a bowl of ice water. Let stand about 10 minutes or until cool; drain. Return asparagus to same bowl. Add cranberry dressing and toss to combine.

Arrange asparagus on 4 serving plates; drizzle with dressing. Top with smoked salmon, some crème fraîche, avocado, more crème fraîche and smoked salmon. Garnish with chives and dill if desired.

Tip
If crème fraîche isn't available, you can substitute with sour cream.

Spring, coho and sockeye salmon, with their higher fat content, have the best flavour when smoked.

Guinness and Maple Prince Edward Island Mussels

Serves 4

Mussels from Prince Edward Island are highly regarded around the world. Since the late 1970s, this indigenous seafood has been actively cultivated to meet consumer demand. In 2001, nearly 18,000 metric tonnes were harvested. Mussels require a great deal of care to cultivate, and they take between 18 months and two years to mature. The mussel larvae are collected from the wild and are suspended on long lines in bays along the coast during their growth, which gives PEI mussels an abundance of fresh food and water, keeping them especially clean. This recipe combines Ireland's favourite brew, PEI's lovely mussels and Canada's favourite syrup.

4 lbs (2 kg) mussels

1/2 cup (125 mL) Guinness

1/2 cup (125 mL) maple syrup

1 Tbsp (15 mL) butter

1/4 cup (60 mL) chopped chives

Scrub mussels under cool running water and remove any beards. Discard mussels that don't close when gently tapped.

Combine Guinness and maple syrup in a large pot and bring to a boil. Add mussels to pot, cover and reduce heat, cooking for about 5 to 6 minutes. Discard any mussels that have not opened. With a slotted spoon, transfer mussels into serving dishes, reserving cooking liquid for use as sauce.

Turn heat to high and bring sauce to a boil. Cook for 2 to 3 minutes, until it has reduced slightly, and whisk in butter. Spoon sauce over mussels, sprinkle with chives and serve hot.

Tip

Use your fresh mussels within 24 hours of bringing them home. The best way to store fresh mussels is to put them in a colander and put the colander in a bowl. Cover the mussels with ice, then a damp towel. The mussels will stay very cold and have good air circulation, but they won't be submerged (and eventually drown) in water.

Arthur Guinness founded his brewery almost 250 years ago in Dublin, Ireland. Guinness stood steadfast through early difficulties, and the company now sells it products around the world. Incidentally, the Guinness family funded the construction of Vancouver's Lion's Gate Bridge in 1937–38, to improve access to their upscale housing development, British Pacific Properties. The bump in the middle of the bridge, sometimes blamed on calculation errors, was actually the result of a tight budget that did not allow for costly curved deck sections.

Malpeque Oysters with Apple and Tobiko Vinaigrette

Serves 8 to 12

Aphrodite sprang from the ocean naked atop an oyster shell, and thus our favourite aphrodisiac was born. Oysters have been cultivated for more than 2000 years, and the Romans apparently fattened up their oysters with wine and pastries. Malpeque oysters come from Prince Edward Island's Malpeque Bay, a corruption of the Mi'kmaq name *Magpeq*, meaning "the swelled up bay." These indigenous shellfish have been cultivated along PEI shores for over a hundred years. They grow in abundance here and have earned a worldwide reputation as the most prized Atlantic oysters. The superior flavour comes from the clean PEI water and the level of saltiness the oyster retains.

pinch of unbleached sugar

juice of 1 lemon

1/2 tsp (2 mL) fresh pepper

1/4 cup (60 mL) finely diced green apple

1/4 cup (60 mL) finely chopped chives

1 oz (28.5 g) jar tobiko (flying fish caviar; see below), divided

1 oz (28.5 g) jar black lumpfish caviar, divided

24 oysters in the shell

crushed ice

2 lemons, cut into wedges

To make vinaigrette, in a small bowl mix together first 5 ingredients plus 1 Tbsp (15 mL) of each caviar, reserving remainder, and set aside.

Shuck oysters, leaving each one in cupped half of its shell. Arrange oyster half-shells on a platter of crushed ice and nestle remaining caviar in centre. Put a teaspoon of vinaigrette on each oyster. Decorate platter with lemon wedges. Serve with remaining vinaigrette, making sure that oysters are kept cool.

Tip
Oysters should be purchased alive and fresh from a reputable source, preferably a store specializing in seafood. The shell should be tightly closed, or, if the shell is slightly open, it should close promptly when tapped. If the shell is open and does not close when tapped, or if the shell is broken, throw the oyster out. Oysters should be stored refrigerated and on ice, covered with a damp cloth, allowing them to breathe.

Tobiko caviar is an inexpensive fish roe that you have probably tried if you eat sushi. It is available in a range of colours, from pale yellow to red, and flavours, such as wasabi. It has a nice pop when you eat it. You can purchase it from a fresh fish market, Japanese specialty food store or on-line.

Digby Scallops with Back Bacon and Vanilla

Serves 4

Digby, Nova Scotia, boasts the best scallops and the largest scallop fishing fleet in the world. Digby scallops are of such high quality because of the clean, cold water in which they grow, and because the Bay of Fundy, with the highest tides in the world, brings in a kaleidoscope of nourishing food. Nine out of 10 of Canada's scallops come from the Digby area. When placed in cold water, fresh-caught scallops will open their shells; in contrast, warm scallops will quite clearly demonstrate the meaning of the saying "clam up." However, unless you live in Digby, the scallops you buy will likely be frozen and out of the shell. Each scallop will have still attached a small muscle that was used to open and close the shell. This muscle is edible, although rather chewy, and you can either leave it on or remove it.

2/3 cup (150 mL) diced back bacon

2 Tbsp (30 mL) minced shallots

1 cup (250 mL) dry champagne

1/2 vanilla bean pod

1/2 tsp (2 mL) champagne vinegar, plus extra for dressing

1 cup (250 mL) cold unsalted butter, cut into small pieces

sea salt and freshly ground white pepper to taste

12 Digby scallops

1 Tbsp (15 mL) olive oil, plus extra for dressing

1 bunch watercress, tough stems removed, cleaned and spun dry

fresh chives for garnish

In a medium saucepan, sauté back bacon until crispy. Set bacon aside and stir in shallots, champagne, vanilla bean pod and seeds, and bring to a boil. Reduce heat to medium-low and simmer until you have about 1/4 cup (60 mL) of liquid remaining. Stir in champagne vinegar and remove vanilla pod. Turn heat down to low and, little by little, whisk in butter, 1 piece at a time. Continue until all butter pieces have been added and sauce will coat back of a spoon dipped in. Stir in bacon, and season sauce with salt and pepper. Keep sauce warm but off direct heat until ready to serve.

Season scallops on all sides with salt and pepper. Place olive oil in a large pan over medium-high heat. When oil is hot, add scallops and sear for 2 to 3 minutes, until nicely caramelized. Turn scallops over and cook for an additional 3 minutes.

For dressing, toss watercress in a bowl with a splash of olive oil and champagne vinegar, and season with salt and pepper. Serve scallops immediately with sauce, watercress and chives.

Tip
To get the most flavour out of a vanilla bean pod, carefully slice it open and scrape out the tiny seeds; use both seeds and pod in the recipe.

What we call "back bacon" is known south of the border and overseas as "Canadian bacon." Praised for its leanness, high quality and smoky flavour, it is the choice bacon for fine hotels and restaurants. Peameal bacon is another extra-lean, very popular Canadian bacon, often roasted whole and served with a maple glaze or sliced and served instead of ham on eggs Benedict.

Winnipeg Goldeye and Crab Cakes

Serves 6

The goldeye *(Hiodon alosoides)* is a small freshwater fish native to waters from the Rockies to Ontario and north to Great Slave Lake. When smoke-cured, it is known as "Winnipeg goldeye." One story of the origin of Winnipeg goldeye is that a Scotsman first smoked the fish when he was lonely for his homeland and for the taste of his favourite fish, kipper. Another story claims that a young man in the 1920s accidentally overcooked his goldeye, and the product later became popular around the world. Most likely, the Native peoples discovered that smoking the fish drastically improved the taste and texture of goldeye, which is unpalatable when fresh. Goldeye was traditionally smoked with readily available, abundant willow wood, but today oak is used for most of the goldeye smoked commercially in Winnipeg. Winnipeg goldeye is still known worldwide for its excellent quality.

3/4 lb (375 g) crabmeat

3/4 lb (375 g) Winnipeg goldeye fillet

1 yellow onion, diced

1 red bell pepper, diced

1 stalk celery, diced

2 Tbsp (30 mL) chopped fresh tarragon

zest from 1 lemon

pinch of cayenne pepper

1 Tbsp (15 mL) Worcestershire sauce

2 tsp (10 mL) Dijon mustard

sea salt and freshly ground black pepper to taste

2 eggs, lightly beaten

seasoned fine breadcrumbs, enough to bind cakes, plus about 3 cups (750 mL) for dredging

flour, seasoned with sea salt and pepper

1 whole egg, beaten, for eggwash

Clean crabmeat, removing all cartilage and shells. Flake goldeye, being sure to remove all bones.

Sauté onion, bell pepper and celery until onion is translucent. Add tarragon, lemon zest, cayenne and Worcestershire sauce to vegetable mixture and let cool to room temperature.

Preheat oven to 375° F (190° C). Mix crabmeat, goldeye, vegetable mixture, Dijon mustard, salt, black pepper and 2 beaten eggs with enough breadcrumbs to hold cakes together. Form into 1/3 cup (75 mL) cakes. Dredge cakes in seasoned flour, then in eggwash and finally in seasoned breadcrumbs.

Pan-fry cakes until golden. Transfer to a baking sheet and finish cooking in oven, about 7 to 10 minutes. Serve hot with chipotle remoulade (see opposite).

Chipotle Remoulade

Chipotles are smoked jalapeño peppers, often found canned in adobe sauce. They are delicious and very spicy. Try the Mexican section at the supermarket, or find a Mexican specialty grocer.

Mix all ingredients together and refrigerate at least 4 hours or up to 1 week.

Tip

For best flavour, the chipotle remoulade must be made at least 4 hours before serving.

Chipotle Remoulade

1 1/2cups (375 mL) mayonnaise

1 Tbsp (15 mL) grainy mustard

chipotle peppers in adobe sauce, minced, about 1 tsp (5 mL) or to taste

1/2 cup (125 mL) finely diced green onions

1 Tbsp (15 mL) chopped capers

1 tsp (5 mL) minced garlic

1/4 cup (60 mL) finely chopped parsley

juice of 1/4 lemon

sea salt and freshly cracked pepper to taste

Panko- and Coconut-crusted Spot Prawns

Serves 6

Spot prawns are named for the distinctive white spots that adorn their shells. Highly regarded for their size and firm, sweet flesh, spot prawns are the largest of the seven shrimp species caught commercially in B.C.'s coastal waters; females are known to grow to 9 inches (23 cm) in length or more. Spot prawns are usually sold fresh for just over 11 weeks beginning in May, mostly in B.C., but they are available frozen year-round. Over 90% of the catch of spot prawns is exported to Japan, although domestic consumption is increasing as more and more Canadian chefs discover the prawns' great taste.

1 cup (250 mL) flour

sea salt and freshly ground pepper

3 eggs

1 cup (250 mL) panko (Japanese bread crumbs)

1/2 cup (125 mL) shredded unsweetened coconut

24 spot prawns, shelled, deveined, tail on

4 cups (1 L) peanut oil, for frying

1/2 cup (125 mL) Thai chili dipping sauce

Place flour in a bowl or shallow baking dish, and season with salt and pepper. Beat eggs in a separate bowl. Combine panko and coconut in another shallow dish. Dredge prawns first in flour, then in beaten eggs and finally coat in panko mixture. Carefully lay prawns out in a single layer on a baking sheet.

Pour oil into a heavy-bottomed skillet and heat to 360° F (180° C); if you do not have a thermometer, test oil with a cube of bread—it should turn golden in under 2 minutes. Cook prawns in small batches until golden, about 2 minutes, then transfer to a plate lined with a paper towel. Serve hot with dipping sauce.

Tip

Whenever possible, buy your prawns with heads on. Keeping them whole is worth the extra work and ensures the flavourful juices are retained in the flesh. Thaw frozen prawns in the refrigerator overnight and use immediately.

Panko is a Japanese-style breadcrumb that is now popular enough to be widely available in most grocery stores (or visit an Asian specialty grocer). It is an ultra-white, extra-coarse breadcrumb that stays particularly crispy when fried.

California Roll

Makes 32 pieces

In the 1970s, Hidekazu Tojo arrived in Vancouver from Japan and found work at one of just four Japanese restaurants in Vancouver at the time. In his desire to entice Canadians' reserved palates into experiencing exotic new foods, Tojo created, among other delights, the now-famous *Tojo-maki*. This hand-held art form was an inside-out version of what would become known as the California roll (attributed to Los Angeles chef Ichiro Manashita). Tojo realized that, by hiding the nori under the rice, Canadians would be more willing to try sushi. He also introduced smoked salmon, a popular Canadian ingredient, into traditional Japanese cuisine and is credited with inventing the popular B.C. roll. Fresh, healthy and delicious, Japanese food plays an integral role in today's Canadian food culture.

1/4 cup (60 mL) rice vinegar

2 Tbsp (30 mL) sugar

2 tsp (10 mL) sea salt

4 cups (1 L) cooked Japanese sushi rice (do not substitute; follow package directions)

bamboo sushi mat

1 package sushi nori (seaweed sheets)

small bowl of lukewarm water with a splash of rice vinegar (to moisten your hands)

mayonnaise or Japanese mayonnaise

2 ripe avocados, peeled, cut into strips and sprinkled with lemon juice

1 large cucumber, peeled, seeded and cut into strips

cooked crabmeat or imitation crab sticks

wasabi, soy sauce and pickled ginger

In a small saucepan over medium heat, combine rice vinegar, sugar and salt. Heat mixture just until sugar dissolves. Remove from heat and let cool.

Place rice in a large bowl and sprinkle vinegar mixture overtop, mixing as you sprinkle. Continue stirring rice gently until it cools. Lay bamboo sushi rolling mat on a cutting board with bamboo strips going horizontally in front of you. Cover mat with plastic wrap and place a sheet of nori on top. Spread about 1 cup (250 mL) rice over 3/4 of nori sheet, leaving approximately 1 inch (2.5 cm) of uncovered nori at near and far ends, dipping your fingers in vinegar water to keep them from sticking to rice.

Spread about 1 Tbsp (15 mL) mayonnaise horizontally along rice. Arrange avocado and cucumber strips along centre of rice and top with crabmeat. Roll sushi, jelly-roll style, rubbing a small amount of water on uncovered edge of nori to help seal it. Gently squeeze rolling mat around sushi roll until it is firm and forms an even roll. Place roll seam side down. Repeat until you have used up rice, making 4 rolls in total.

Cut each roll into 8 pieces. Serve rolls at room temperature with wasabi, soy sauce and pickled ginger.

Tip
Wet the knife between each cut to keep the rice from sticking to it.

Inside-out Rolls
After spreading rice on nori, sprinkle with roasted sesame seeds. Cover with a second sheet of plastic wrap. Lifting with bottom plastic wrap, turn nori and rice over onto bamboo rolling mat (nori-side up). Remove top plastic wrap and proceed as per recipe.

Smoked Trout and Green Onion Basil Cakes

Serves 6

At the easternmost tip of North America, what we now call Newfoundland and Labrador have naturally been the first ports of landing for many explorers from Europe throughout the centuries. The first to visit, over a thousand years ago, are believed to have been Icelandic Vikings who went off course. Subsequent Vikings built several settlements but are thought to have stayed only a few decades. Although Iberian fisherman eventually discovered the rich fishing grounds of the Grand Banks in the 1400s, it was not until John Cabot's voyage of 1497 that word spread to other European countries. In recent years, overfishing and loss of habitat have reduced fish populations in most areas, but Labrador still boasts brook trout as large as footballs, making it a world-class destination for anglers.

3 cups (750 mL) flour

1 cup (250 mL) warm water

2 tsp (10 mL) sea salt

1/2 tsp (2 mL) cayenne or crushed chilies

1 tsp (5 mL) Thai fish sauce

1/4 cup (60 mL) grapeseed oil, plus about 1/2 cup (125 mL) for frying

toasted sesame oil for brushing cakes, about 1/4 cup (60 mL)

1 1/4 cups (310 mL) chopped green onions

1 cup (250 mL) chopped fresh basil, reserving some for garnish

cream cheese, about 1 cup (250 mL)

1 lb (500 g) smoked trout, thinly sliced

Combine flour, water, salt, cayenne, fish sauce and 1/4 cup (60 mL) grapeseed oil together in a bowl and mix to form a dough. Knead on a floured surface for about 5 minutes, until smooth. Cover with plastic wrap and let rest for 20 minutes.

Roll dough into a cylinder and cut into 12 equal pieces. Working quickly, roll first piece into a 4-inch (10 cm) circle. Brush with a little sesame oil and sprinkle with green onions and basil. Roll once again, like a jelly roll, then coil roll into a circle. Roll circle out to a 4-inch (10 cm) circle and continue with remaining dough.

Heat 2 Tbsp (30 mL) grapeseed oil in a medium skillet and fry each cake separately until golden, adding more oil as needed to fry all cakes.

To serve, place a dollop of cream cheese on each cake and top with slices of smoked trout. Garnish with fresh basil.

Tip
The green onion basil cakes can be stored, well wrapped and frozen, for up to 2 months. They can be reheated in a low oven (200° F [90° C]) for about 5 minutes.

This recipe would be equally delicious if you used any smoked fish, such as smoked salmon or tuna, instead of the trout. Without the basil, the green onion cakes resemble the ones of Chinese cuisine—serve with a spicy soy, ginger and sesame oil sauce or sambal oelek (Indonesian red chili paste).

Spanakopita

Makes about 16 triangles

Canada's first Greek immigrants, fleeing difficult conditions surrounding the 1821 revolution in their homeland, settled in Montréal and Vancouver. The main wave of Greeks came to Canada after World War II, peaking in the late 1960s; there are now upwards of 250,000 Greeks in Canada. The Greek community in Canada has held fast to its traditions and language, mostly thanks to the strong influence of the Greek Orthodox Church, with dozens of parishes dotted across the country. Greek festivals are held annually in a number of cities, including Toronto, Vancouver, Ottawa and Calgary. Our Greek immigrants have enriched Canada in many ways, not the least of which has been introducing their delicious and easily recognizable cuisine, whose roots are based in antiquity.

1/3 cup (75 mL) butter

1/3 cup (75 mL) flour

2 cups (500 mL) whole milk

1/2 tsp (2 mL) nutmeg

pinch of sea salt

freshly ground pepper to taste

3 lbs (1.5 kg) fresh spinach, washed

3 cups (750 mL) Greek feta cheese

juice of 1/2 lemon

dill and chopped green onion (optional)

1 package Greek phyllo pastry

unsalted butter, melted, for brushing (approximately 1 cup [250 mL])

In a small pot, melt 1/3 cup (75 mL) butter. Stir in flour and cook over low heat for 5 minutes. Scald milk in another pan and pour into butter and flour, stirring and cooking for 10 minutes until you have a smooth, thick sauce. Season with nutmeg, salt and pepper and set aside.

Bring a large pot of water to a boil. Cook spinach for 1 minute, then plunge into ice water. Drain and squeeze out as much moisture as possible. Chop spinach and place in a large bowl. Crumble feta on top. Pour sauce over spinach and feta, and add lemon juice. Stir well and adjust seasonings. Dill and green onion are popular additions that can be incorporated at this stage.

Preheat oven to 400° F (200° C). To prevent them from drying and becoming brittle, cover the stack of phyllo sheets with a clean, damp kitchen towel as you work. Place 1 sheet of phyllo on a work surface with short side facing you and brush with melted butter. Fold phyllo into thirds, lengthwise. Place a heaping tablespoon of spinach mixture near corner of strip nearest you, and then fold pastry over filling to form a triangle. Continue to fold pastry around filling, ending with seam on bottom. Place triangles on a parchment-lined baking sheet and brush with butter. Continue to make spanakopita until filling is all used. Bake until golden brown, about 15 minutes.

Tip
Spanakopita can be made ahead and stored, well wrapped and refrigerated, for up to 2 days. Alternatively, they can be arranged in single layers in freezer bags and kept for up to 2 months. Bake frozen spanakopita (do not thaw) in the same manner as above, adjusting the cooking time to about 20 to 25 minutes.

Smoky Beef Jerky (and Pemmican)

Makes about 35 pieces

Pemmican is a high-energy food ration developed by First Nations and adopted by the earliest settlers and Hudson's Bay Company voyageurs. Meat, mostly bison, was dried and pounded almost to a flour, then mixed with animal fat and—if you were lucky—dried berries, for flavour. Traditional pemmican was not very tasty, but it didn't spoil and travelled well as a convenient source of protein. Today, we mostly eat dried meat as jerky. Homemade jerky is fantastic and can be seasoned to your preference. It is a delicious, dense form of protein that doesn't spoil and travels well—an excellent substitute for pemmican.

1/3 cup (75 mL) soy sauce

1/4 cup (60 mL) Bourbon whisky

1/4 cup (60 mL) brown sugar, packed

1/4 cup (60 mL) white vinegar

2 Tbsp (30 mL) Worcestershire sauce

1 Tbsp (15 mL) chili powder

1 Tbsp (15 mL) garlic powder

2 tsp (10 mL) Louisiana hot sauce

2 tsp (10 mL) pepper

1 lb (500 g) flank steak, trimmed of fat, thinly sliced across the grain into 1/8 inch (3 mm) slices

For the marinade, combine the first 9 ingredients in a medium bowl.

Put the beef into a large resealable freezer bag and pour the marinade over top. Seal the bag and turn until the meat is well coated. Marinate in the fridge for at least 6 hours or overnight, turning occasionally.

Remove the beef from the bag and discard any remaining marinade. Preheat your smoking device to 200°F (95°C) using hickory wood. Arrange the beef evenly on a rack that will fit in your smoker, and smoke for about 2 hours, until the beef is dried but still flexible. Cool completely.

Butter-poached Prince Edward Island Lobster Tails with Beet Coulis

Serves 4

At the beginning of the 19th century, lobster was considered "poor people's food," and children in the Maritimes were mocked for bringing lobster sandwiches to school. New Brunswick even had a regulation that forbade parents from sending lobster sandwiches more than twice per week. Lobster eventually lost its stigma, but the traditional drying and salting methods used for preserving fish did not work on the delicate meat; it perished quickly and was unsuitable for export. Widespread interest in lobster came with the introduction of canning in the mid-1800s, which allowed the meat to be preserved and exported. Then, in 1927, the first shipment of live lobsters was sent by rail to the United States, and, except during the Depression in the 1930s, the lobster industry has steadily increased. Live lobster can now be found in the markets of most Canadian communities. Canada is the world's largest source of *Homarus americanus* or "true" lobster, and Prince Edward Island is arguably the best place to get it.

1/4 cup (60 mL) white wine vinegar

1/4 cup (60 mL) sea salt

pot of boiling water, large enough to hold lobsters

4 x 2 lb (1 kg) whole, fresh, live lobsters

bowl of ice water, large enough to hold lobsters

1 cup (250 mL) beet juice (see Tip)

1 star anise, whole

4 peppercorns

1/2 tsp (2 mL) balsamic vinegar

1/2 cup (125 mL) light fish stock

1 lb (454 g) butter

pumpkin seed oil for garnish

Add vinegar and salt to boiling water. Plunge lobsters into pot and cook, covered, for 4 minutes; remove from pot and immerse in ice water for 10 minutes. Separate tail meat from lobster and set aside. (Reserve remaining lobster meat for another use.)

To make beet coulis, heat beet juice with star anise and peppercorns over medium heat until reduced and thick. Strain coulis and stir in balsamic vinegar. Set aside.

Heat fish stock in a medium pan and reduce to about 2 Tbsp (30 mL). Meanwhile, cut butter into small cubes. When stock has reduced, lower heat and whisk in butter, 1 cube at a time, until all used and sauce is thick. Place butter sauce over medium-low heat, being careful not to let it boil. Poach lobster tails in butter sauce until done but not overcooked, about 6 minutes.

Serve over steamed white asparagus or sautéed spinach with slices of cooked beets, beet coulis and a drizzle of pumpkin seed oil.

Tip
If you have a juicer, you can make your own beet juice. Alternatively, you can buy it from your local juice bar or buy a bottled concentrate, available in many European stores.

Atlantic Boiled Lobster
Maritimers assert that the only way to cook lobster is to put it into a large pot with boiling, salty seawater, a decidedly Canadian technique. Other than that, all you need is butter. On the Prairies, a large pot of water and a healthy addition of sea salt will do. Either way, cook each lobster 5 minutes per pound, and serve with fresh lemon and melted butter or a butter sauce.

Duck Confit with Caramelized Rutabaga and Risotto

Serves 10

Duck confit is simply duck that has been salt cured and poached in its own fat until it is very tender. Ducks were an important source of protein for First Nations and early settlers, and duck hunting is still a popular fall pastime. Duck and wild rice dinner is especially popular on the Prairies, where the combination of the two is readily available: where the wild rice grows, you will also find ducks. In this recipe, duck is paired instead with risotto, a dish made with Arborio rice and an Italian favourite enjoyed by many Canadians. Rutabagas, a fall vegetable with an earthy, sweet flavour, round out the meal.

10 duck legs

2 heads garlic, halved crosswise

1 lemon, sliced into about 5 rings

1 orange, sliced into about 5 rings

1/2 cinnamon stick

4 star anise, whole

1 tsp (5 mL) black peppercorns, whole

1/2 inch (12 mm) fresh ginger, sliced into three pieces

6 sprigs of fresh thyme

3 bay leaves

1/2 lb (250 g) kosher salt

about 2 lbs (1 kg) of rendered duck fat and 4 cups (1 L) grape seed or olive oil

Rutabaga

2 Tbsp (30 mL) butter

2 Tbsp (30 mL) brown sugar

2 small rutabagas, peeled, quartered and sliced, 1/4 inch (6 mm) thick

sea salt and freshly ground pepper to taste

Layer the duck legs, garlic halves, lemon and orange slices, spices and herbs, in a nonreactive container, generously sprinkling with salt between each layer. Cover with plastic wrap, and cure in refrigerator for 24 hours.

Preheat the oven to 250° F (120° C). Remove the duck legs and pat them dry (you can rinse them if you prefer a milder salt flavour). Rinse and drain garlic, fruit, spices and herbs. Place duck legs and fruit mixture, alternating layers, into a deep baking dish and cover with the duck fat and oil. Bake for 6 to 8 hours or until the meat is very tender.

To prepare the rutabaga, heat butter and brown sugar in a small pan until butter is melted. Add rutabaga slices and cook over medium heat until tender, about 12 to 15 minutes. Season with salt and pepper and set aside.

Tip
If you don't plan to serve the duck right away, allow it to cool before transferring into a crock or plastic container. Strain the fat through a fine sieve, and pour enough over the meat to cover. Once the duck legs have cooled completely, they can be stored in the refrigerator for up to three months.

For the risotto, melt butter in a skillet over medium heat and sauté onion until softened but not coloured, about 5 minutes. Add the rice and sauté for 2 to 4 minutes, stirring to coat the grains. Then add the white wine. Stir to combine until it is absorbed, about 3 minutes. Add a ladle of the hot broth, stirring slowly but continuously, until it is almost completely absorbed by the rice. Continue adding broth until all of it is absorbed and the rice is tender but slightly chewy and very creamy. This will take about 25 minutes. Stir in the remaining 1 Tbsp (15 mL) of butter, parsley and Parmesan cheese. Add salt and pepper to taste. Serve the risotto piping hot with the duck confit and caramelized rutabaga.

Risotto

1/4 cup (60 mL) unsalted butter, plus 1 Tbsp (15 mL) to finish

1/4 cup (60 mL) onion, chopped

2 cups (500 mL) Arborio rice

1/2 cup (125 mL) white wine

5 cups (1.25 L) hot chicken or vegetable broth

1/4 cup (60 mL) parsley, chopped

1/2 cup (125 mL) grated Parmesan cheese

sea salt and freshly ground pepper to taste

Cedar-planked Salmon with Orange Pistachio Crust

Serves 4

Abundant year-round and easily harvested along spawning routes, salmon were traditionally a key resource for West Coast First Nations. Equally abundant and important were the cedar trees on the coast. It made sense for the Natives to cook their freshly caught salmon on easily split cedar planks. They filleted the salmon and cooked it skin-side down, secured to the plank with saplings. The Natives then propped the plank at an angle above the fire, thus perfuming the meat with a delicate, smoky flavour. The traditional preparation would have simply included the salmon and the cedar, perhaps with some wild herbs. We have added a crust that adds depth of flavour without overpowering the delicate salmon. Wild-caught salmon, if you can get it, is recommended. The same method can be used with other kinds of fish, such as arctic char, and with aromatic hardwoods, such as maple, but never use treated wood.

1 cup (250 mL) unsalted, shelled pistachios, chopped

2/3 cup (150 mL) panko (see p. 37)

2 Tbsp (30 mL) olive oil

1 Tbsp (15 mL) chopped fresh dill

2 tsp (10 mL) Dijon mustard

zest from 1 orange

1/4 cup (60 mL) orange juice

4 x 8 oz (250 g) skin-on salmon fillets, any species

2 cedar planks (see Tip)

sea salt and pepper to taste

Preheat grill to medium-high. Mix pistachios and panko together—it works especially well to pulse them together in a food processor. Place on a plate and set aside.

Mix oil, dill, mustard, zest and orange juice to form a paste. Spread paste evenly on flesh side of each salmon fillet, then dip in pistachio and panko mixture. As they are crusted, lay the fillets skin-side down on prepared planks. Season crust with sea salt and freshly ground pepper. Place planks on grill, close lid and cook 12 to 15 minutes.

Tip
Purchase untreated cedar planks, 1 inch (2.5 cm) thick, 8 inches (20 cm) wide and 12 inches (30 cm) long, from your local lumberyard or gourmet shop or barbecue supply store. The planks must be soaked in water for a minimum of 1 hour, but 4 to 6 hours is best. Drain and pat dry; brush with oil before using.

Experiment with the crust mixture for this recipe or for use with other fish, chicken or meats. A blend of fresh chopped herbs works especially well, or you can add dried, chopped fruit such as apricots or cranberries. For added crunchiness, substitute cornmeal for some of the breadcrumbs.

Traditional Hungarian Goulash with Sage Dumplings

Serves 6

Searching for land and opportunity, Hungarians began coming to Canada in the 1880s. Immigration agent "Count" Paul Esterhazy established colonies in what is now Saskatchewan; until 1956, Canada's largest concentration of Hungarians was in this province's Qu'Appelle Valley. The centre of Hungarian Canadian culture eventually moved to Winnipeg, with a strong Hungarian presence in Toronto, Montreal, Windsor, Brantford and Hamilton. The word "goulash" comes from the Hungarian *gúlyas*, which means "herdsman" and also connotes a stew, easily prepared and reheated for many days, that originated in the 9th century. Although every Hungarian family has its own version of this simple, tasty dish, there are two cardinal rules for an authentic *gúlyas:* no flour and no tomatoes! The rich colour comes from generous amounts of Hungarian paprika, and the traditional thickening agent is potato.

3 lbs (1.5 kg) beef outside round or sirloin tip, diced

3/4 cup (175 mL) sweet Hungarian paprika

1/4 cup (60 mL) sunflower or grapeseed oil

4 large onions, diced

2 heads garlic (about 12 cloves), minced

5 potatoes, peeled and diced

brown beef stock to cover

sea salt and pepper to taste

Sage Dumplings
1 1/2 cups (375 mL) flour

1/2 cup (125 mL) cornmeal

1 Tbsp (15 mL) baking powder

1/2 tsp (2 mL) sea salt

2 Tbsp (30 mL) minced fresh sage

1 1/4 cups (310 mL) half and half cream (18%) or buttermilk

Roll diced beef in paprika to coat. In a large pot or Dutch oven, brown beef with oil and onions, taking time to brown it nicely. Add garlic and potatoes, cover with stock and bring to a boil. Immediately reduce heat and gently simmer, semi-covered, skimming fat from surface regularly, until meat is tender, about 1 hour. Season with salt and pepper to taste. Meanwhile, make dumplings.

Sift first 4 ingredients into a bowl. Stir in sage and add cream, stirring just to combine. Drop dough a teaspoon at a time into hot goulash as prepared above. Cover and cook 8 to 10 minutes or until a toothpick inserted into centre comes out clean.

Tip
Goulash is better the next day because the flavours will have had a chance to mingle and develop. If you are planning to serve it to company, prepare it a day or two ahead of time and simply reheat, make the dumplings and serve. The goulash also freezes well (add dumplings just before serving) for up to 1 month.

Sweet and Sour Pork

Serves 6

Chinese immigrants began to settle in British Columbia in good numbers beginning with the Fraser River Gold Rush of 1858. Many found work as cooks in mining and logging camps, despite the fact that few if any of them were trained chefs. The Chinese smorgasbord originated in Vancouver around 1870, when Swedish mill workers convinced Chinese cooks to let them load their plates from a steam table containing all the various dishes. Immigrants from China have continued to come to Canada, often in the face of great hardship. Today, the Chinese are the largest visible ethnic group in Vancouver, and highly regarded Chinese restaurants are found across the country, many of which feature a Chinese buffet that includes sweet and sour pork.

2 Tbsp (30 mL) cornstarch

1 Tbsp (15 mL) cold water

1 lb (500 g) boneless pork loin rib, cut into bite-sized pieces

2 egg yolks

1 Tbsp (15 mL) soy sauce

2 tsp (5 mL) sea salt, divided

2/3 cup (150 mL) rice wine vinegar

1/4 cup (60 mL) white wine

1/3 cup (75 mL) sugar

3 cloves garlic, minced

2 Tbsp (30 mL) grated fresh ginger

1/2 small pineapple, peeled, cored, quartered and sliced

1 small tomato, diced

1/2 cup (125 mL) julienned red bell pepper

1 tsp (5 mL) cinnamon

vegetable oil for frying

1/4 cup (60 mL) each cornstarch and flour, sifted together into a bowl

1 cup (250 mL) snow peas

In a bowl, add cornstarch to cold water and mix well. Add pork, egg yolks, soy sauce and 1 tsp (5 mL) salt. Toss well, and refrigerate overnight.

Place vinegar, wine, sugar and remaining 1 tsp (5 mL) salt into a pan and bring to a boil. Add garlic and ginger; reduce heat and simmer for 10 minutes. Add pineapple, tomato, bell pepper and cinnamon and simmer an additional 10 minutes or until tomato becomes incorporated into sauce. Remove from heat and set sauce aside.

Heat oil to 350° F (175° C) to fry pork. Toss marinated pork in flour and cornstarch mixture and fry in hot oil until cooked, about 5 minutes. Drain well on kitchen towel. Heat sauce through, adding snow peas just before serving. Spoon sauce over pork and serve with rice or noodles.

Tip
Try this dish with other meats, such as chicken or beef; it also works well with tofu. The sauce can be made up to 3 days ahead and stored in the fridge.

Salt Spring Island Lamb with Mustard Spaetzle

Serves 4

Canada is the world's largest exporter of mustard seed and has been among the world's top producers since World War II—a great business, considering over 700 million pounds (32 thousand metric tonnes) of mustard are used worldwide each year. Canada's mustard production started in 1936 with 100 acres (40 ha) in southern Alberta, and over time, it spread across the Prairies. Today, most of Canada's mustard is grown in Saskatchewan, and over 75% of the yield is exported. Salt Spring Island lamb is internationally renowned, and Queen Elizabeth is said to prefer it to other lamb. The best theory as to why it tastes superior is that salt water from the ocean travels inland on the wind and settles on the grass the sheep eat. It is also well known that Salt Spring Island sheep are fed on a diet, well, fit for a queen.

2 x 1 1/2 lbs (750 g) lamb racks, frenched (trimmed and ready to use; available in most grocery stores)

2 Tbsp (30 mL) extra virgin olive oil

sea salt and freshly ground pepper

1 clove garlic, minced

1 cup (250 mL) chopped fresh parsley

2 Tbsp (30 mL) each chopped fresh thyme and rosemary

1/4 cup (60 mL) breadcrumbs

1/4 cup (60 mL) Dijon mustard

Spaetzle
1 1/4 cups (310 mL) flour

1 tsp (5 mL) sea salt

3 large eggs

1/3 cup (75 mL) milk

1 Tbsp (15 mL) grainy Dijon mustard

Place a heavy-bottomed pan over medium-high heat. Brush lamb with oil and season with salt and pepper. Sear lamb until brown on all sides. Remove from heat and let sit 15 minutes.

Preheat oven to 450° F (230° C). Mix garlic and herbs together in a bowl with breadcrumbs. Place lamb on a small, rimmed baking sheet; brush Dijon on rounded side of lamb. Divide breadcrumb mixture evenly over chops, covering mustard to form a crust. Bake for 10 to 15 minutes or until a thermometer inserted in centre reaches 140° F (60° C) for medium rare. Let rest 5 to 10 minutes before cutting into chops. Serve with spaetzle (below).

Bring a large pot of salted water to a boil. Set a bowl of ice water near pot. Sift flour and salt together. Whisk together eggs, milk and Dijon and pour into flour, stirring to make a smooth batter. Using a spaetzle maker or food mill, drop batter into boiling water. When spaetzle come to surface, transfer them to ice water with a slotted spoon. Repeat until all batter is used. As they cool, remove spaetzle from water and place in sieve to drain. To reheat spaetzle, toss them in hot butter or sauce—or fry them over medium heat until golden.

Spaetzle or spätzle ("little sparrow") are German dumplings very similar to pasta. They are served as a side dish and are common fare, especially in southern Germany and the Alsace region. Spaetzle makers are available at specialty food shops, department stores and German markets (where you will likely find a good one for a reasonable price).

Deep Dish Tourtière

Serves 8 to 10

One theory for the origin of this French Canadian dish's name suggests that tourtière was previously made with now-extinct passenger pigeons *(tourtes)*. However, it was more likely named for a type of pie pan dating back to medieval France that was used to cook on the hearth. The traditional spice blend—cinnamon, nutmeg, cloves and allspice—is also French in origin. There is no agreement on the "traditional" meats to use—or whether they should be ground or chopped—but a true Québec tourtière should definitely have a bottom and top crust. My favourite is a double-crusted blend of ground beef, pork and chicken served with ketchup, but you can also serve it with a green tomato relish.

Pastry (enough for 2 crusts)
4 1/2 cups (1.1 L) flour

1 Tbsp (15 mL) baking powder

2 tsp (10 mL) sea salt

1 lb (454 g) unsalted butter

1 cup (250 mL) hot water

juice of 1/2 lemon

2 eggs, 1 for pastry and 1 beaten for eggwash

Filling
4 medium yellow onions, diced

2 Tbsp (30 mL) unsalted butter

1 lb (500 g) ground pork

1 lb (500 g) ground beef OR lamb

2 large baking potatoes, grated

1 Tbsp (15 mL) minced garlic

1/2 bottle red wine

2 Tbsp (30 mL) chopped fresh rosemary

1/4 cup (60 mL) balsamic vinegar

1 tsp (5 mL) ground allspice

1 tsp (5 mL) cinnamon

Sift dry ingredients into a food processor. Melt 2/3 cup (150 mL) butter in hot water and let cool. Pulse remaining butter into flour mixture until it resembles coarse meal. Whisk 1 egg and lemon juice into butter and water and pour into processor, pulsing until just coming together. Form into 2 discs, one slightly larger than other. Wrap and chill for at least 2 hours.

In a large pot, brown onions in butter, then add meats. Brown meat, stirring to break up clumps. Add remaining ingredients and simmer uncovered for 20 minutes or until starting to thicken. Remove from heat and set aside to cool.

Preheat oven to 375° F (190° C). Roll out larger disk and line a 9-inch (23 cm) springform pan with it. Brush pastry with egg wash, pour in cooled filling and cover with top crust. Slash top to allow steam to escape, brush with egg wash and bake until golden brown, 30 to 40 minutes.

Tip
Make the pastry up to 2 days in advance and store it, well wrapped, in the refrigerator. Let it sit out of the fridge for 10 minutes before rolling. Purchased pastry can also be used.

Acadian Shepherd's Pie

Serves 6

While growing up, many Canadian children with Acadian roots enjoyed *pâté chinois* as a staple dinner offering. This dish hailed from Ireland and was traditionally prepared with lamb. One explanation for the origin of the name *pâté chinois* is as follows. Between 1755 and 1763, the British forcibly expelled up to 18,000 Acadians from the former French colony of Acadia in the Maritimes. After being jam-packed into pitch-dark ship holds, the survivors scattered widely, settling in locations such as Louisiana (where they gave rise to Cajun culture) and Maine. When Québeckers went to the U.S. in the late 19th century to work in mills, they brought the dish back with them from the town of China, Maine, where the resettled Acadians had introduced it.

2 medium yellow onions, minced

1/2 cup (125 mL) unsalted butter, plus 3 Tbsp (45 mL), with extra for dotting

1 1/2 lbs (750 g) ground beef

1 Tbsp (15 mL) Worcestershire sauce

1 cup (250 mL) diced red bell pepper

1 Tbsp (15 mL) minced garlic

1/2 cup (125 mL) rich beef stock

2 cups (500 mL) creamed corn (see opposite) or 1 x 540 mL can creamed corn

2 eggs, separated

1/2 cup (125 mL) heavy cream (32%)

6 large potatoes, boiled and mashed

Preheat oven to 375° F (190° C). In a pan on stove, sauté onions in 3 Tbsp (45 mL) butter until golden. Add beef and brown well. Add Worcestershire sauce, bell pepper, garlic and stock, stirring to combine. Remove from heat.

Grease a 9 x 11-inch (23 x 28 cm) casserole dish and spread beef in it; top with creamed corn.

Stir 1/2 cup (125 mL) butter, egg yolks and cream into mashed potatoes. Whip egg whites to soft peaks and fold into potato mixture. Spread potato mixture over creamed corn layer and dot with butter. Bake for 25 to 30 minutes to heat through. Then broil until potatoes brown, 2 to 3 minutes.

Creamed Corn

Scrape kernels off cobs. Melt butter in a pan and sauté corn kernels until cooked (with onion, garlic or wine if desired), about 5 minutes. Season with salt and pepper, and pour in cream. Simmer until thick.

Creamed Corn

3 cobs corn

1 Tbsp (15 mL) butter

minced onion, garlic, splash of white wine (optional)

sea salt and pepper to taste

approximately 1/2 cup (125 mL) heavy cream (32%)

Cod au Gratin with Sauce Bercy

Serves 4

Portuguese and Basque hook-and-line cod fishermen came to the waters off what is now Canada as early as the 1400s. They would arrive in spring and return to their home ports in fall. To preserve the cod until it reached the markets of Europe, it was dried and salted. Fishermen from other countries discovered the cod stocks as well; by the late 1500s, the British were processing their catch onshore in Newfoundland, whereas the French preferred to salt theirs aboard their ship. Cod became an early staple of Atlantic Canadian cuisine. The original cod au gratin was topped with breadcrumbs, but legend has it that a chef at a hotel in St. John's, finding no bread-crumbs in the pantry, substituted grated cheese—thereby creating a winner. Cod were once so abundant in the area that what is now Newfoundland was for a time called Baccalaos (after the Portuguese word for salted cod), but unchecked overfish-ing caused a devastating crash in cod populations by the 1990s.

1 lb (500 g) fresh cod fillets

1/4 cup (60 mL) dry white wine

1 Tbsp (15 mL) lemon zest

juice of 1/2 lemon

1 tsp (5 mL) sea salt

1/4 tsp (1 mL) chili flakes

1/4 cup (60 mL) butter, divided

1 Tbsp (15 mL) flour

2 egg yolks

2 Tbsp (30 mL) heavy cream (32%)

2 Tbsp (30 mL) grated Parmesan cheese

fresh dill for garnish

Sauce Bercy (named for the historical Bercy region of Paris) is a roux-thickened, fish-based sauce, a variation of the classic velouté sauce, one of the mother sauces of French cuisine.

Preheat oven to 400° F (200° C). Place cod in a single layer in a buttered, shallow baking dish. Sprinkle with wine, lemon zest and juice, salt and chili flakes. Dot with 1 Tbsp (15 mL) of butter, cover tightly and bake for 10 minutes or until fish is cooked.

Drain liquid from dish, reserving 1 cup (250 mL). In a small saucepan, melt remaining butter and stir in flour. Cook for 5 minutes, stirring, then add reserved fish stock and cook until smooth and thick, about 7 minutes.

In a small bowl, whisk together egg yolks and cream. Add a few tablespoons of hot fish sauce to temper eggs, then pour egg mixture into saucepan with fish sauce to heat through, about 1 minute. Spoon sauce over cod and sprinkle with Parmesan cheese. Broil until golden, about 4 minutes. Serve with fresh dill, rice or mashed potatoes and a side salad.

Tip
For a gourmet touch, place sliced, cooked lobster, crab or shrimp on top of the cod before adding the sauce and broiling. You could also add a sprinkle of fresh herbs, such as dill or tarragon, to the sauce. For extra crunch, stir 2 Tbsp (30 mL) fine breadcrumbs into the grated Parmesan cheese before broiling.

Wild Rice Pilaf

Serves 4

The only cereal native to Canada, wild rice is the seed of aquatic grasses (*Zizania* spp.) rather than a member of the rice family. Eaten by people since prehistoric times, it has been harvested by canoe for centuries throughout the Great Lakes region and the Prairies. Its importance is evident in the name it was given by the Algonquins and related First Nations: *manomin* (or *minomin*) means "the good seed" or "the good berry." Difficulties in cultivating and harvesting wild rice, as well as its limited supply, have made it one of the most expensive and desired varieties of rice in the world. Saskatchewan supplies nearly 70% of the annual harvest, which typically ranges from 850 to 2700 metric tonnes.

1 cup (250 mL) diced slab bacon

1 large onion, diced

2 cups (500 mL) sliced mushrooms, preferably wild

1 clove garlic, minced

1 cup (250 mL) canned Italian Roma tomatoes

1 Tbsp (15 mL) chopped fresh thyme

3 cups (750 mL) cooked wild rice (see below)

2/3 cup (150 mL) heavy cream (32%)

salt and pepper to taste

1/3 cup (75 mL) grated pecorino cheese

Simple Wild Rice

1 cup (250 mL) wild rice, rinsed and drained

boiling water to cover

1 Tbsp (15 mL) sea salt

butter and fresh herbs such as thyme, sage and parsley (optional)

Preheat oven to 350° F (175° C). In a large skillet, fry bacon until starting to crisp and some fat has been rendered. Set bacon aside and drain all but 3 Tbsp (45 mL) of fat from skillet. Fry onion and mushrooms in skillet until both begin to caramelize and liquid from mushrooms has evaporated. Add bacon, garlic, tomatoes, thyme and rice to skillet and simmer for 5 minutes. Pour in cream, heat through and season with salt and pepper. Pour into a buttered baking dish and top with cheese. Bake until golden, about 15 minutes.

Simple Wild Rice
Cover wild rice with boiling water and let sit 5 minutes. Drain, repeat soaking and drain again to tame any strong weedy flavours. Cover rice with fresh cold water, add sea salt, bring to a boil and simmer for 30 to 45 minutes, until tender. Drain. At this point you can add rice to your favourite recipe or serve it with butter and freshly chopped herbs.

Roasted Turkey

Serves 8 to 10

Roasted turkey, usually stuffed with a family-recipe stuffing, is a tried-and-true traditional dish for Canadian Thanksgiving dinner. Wild turkeys still roam over much of southern Canada, although the ones in Ontario were reintroduced after being wiped out of that province by overhunting and loss of habitat. Most turkey consumed in Canada today is of the domesticated variety, namely the Broad-breasted White, an over-hybridized, top-heavy breed. For a different, some say superior flavour, seek out heritage breeds such as the Bourbon Red, Standard Bronze and Ridley Bronze, Canada's own heritage breed.

1 x 12 lb (6 kg) turkey, fresh or thawed completely, if frozen

sea salt and freshly ground pepper

1 to 2 cups (250 to 500 mL) water or chicken broth (optional)

Preheat oven to 450° F (230° C). Set turkey out at room temperature for 45 minutes. Remove neck, giblets and any fat from cavity. Rinse turkey, pat dry with paper towels and season well with lots of salt and pepper. Place in a roasting pan and roast for 1 3/4 to 2 hours, or until a thermometer inserted into the thickest part of the thigh reads 170° F (77° C) and the juices run clear. Check the turkey after 1 hour, and if drippings are becoming too dark, add 1 to 2 cups (250 to 500 mL) of water or chicken broth into the pan. Remove the roasted turkey from the oven and let it rest for at least 20 minutes before carving.

Arctic Char with Zucchini Noodles and Avocado Mousse

Serves 4

A member of the salmon family, the arctic char (*Salvelinus alpinus*) is a pink-fleshed fish known as *iqaluk* or *ilkalupik* by the Inuit. It has the northernmost distribution of any freshwater fish. Most char live within the Arctic Circle, although a few populations in North America and Asia were landlocked during the last Ice Age. Char have always been important to the diet of the Inuit peoples, who trap them in a stone weir and spear them with a traditional spear, the *kakivak*. Fresh char is usually available from a good seafood retailer, especially if you call ahead and reserve. Arctic char can be used in place of salmon or trout in any recipe.

1 cup (250 mL) heavy cream (32%)

2 ripe avocados

juice of 2 lemons, reserving 2 Tbsp (30 mL)

sea salt and freshly ground pepper

8 small yellow and green zucchini, sliced lengthwise thinly to make "noodles" (use vegetable peeler)

1/2 small red onion, thinly sliced

1/3 cup (75 mL) extra virgin olive oil, plus additional for cooking

1/4 cup (60 mL) chopped fresh dill

2 x 2 lb (1 kg) arctic char fillets, each portioned into 2 pieces

Whip cream to a soft peak; cover and chill while preparing avocados. Remove flesh from avocados, add lemon juice and mash with a fork. Using back of a spoon, press avocado mash through a fine sieve into a clean bowl. Fold in whipped cream, season with salt and pepper, cover and refrigerate. Avocado mousse can be made up to 3 hours ahead.

Preheat oven to 400° F (200° C). Toss zucchini "noodles" and onion with olive oil, dill and reserved lemon juice. Season with salt and pepper and set aside.

Heat a heavy-bottomed, ovenproof pan over high heat. Sprinkle arctic char with olive oil and season well with salt and pepper. Sear fish, skin-side down, until crispy, about 1 minute. Place pan in oven and bake fish until cooked, 3 to 5 minutes depending on thickness of fish.

Arrange zucchini onto 4 plates and top each with a fillet of char. Spoon avocado mousse overtop and serve.

Also known as "alligator pear," the avocado is, like the tomato and cucumber, a fruit that is most often used as a vegetable. Originally from Mexico and Central America, it has been hailed as an aphrodisiac for centuries. Avocados are most often sold unripe, so buy them a day or two before you need them. For best flavour, store avocados at room temperature. To speed up ripening, put them in a paper bag with an apple and leave overnight.

Cabbage Rolls

Serves 4

Cooks love to make little packages of food for their families, and cabbage leaves lend themselves particularly well to this task. Because cabbage rolls appear in so many cuisines, spanning continents, languages and centuries, it is difficult to pin down their origin. Many Canadians have fond memories of a kitchen full of women—from multiple generations of a family—making dozens and dozens of delicious cabbage rolls for an upcoming holiday or special gathering. These cabbage rolls are of Ukrainian origin, a nod to the large numbers of Ukrainians who came to settle the Canadian prairie beginning in the early 1890s. No matter their ethnic origin, cabbage rolls make a frugal and filling meal.

1 1/2 cups (375 mL) rice

2 cups (500 mL) vegetable or chicken stock for rice AND 2 cups (500 mL) or more stock for cooking cabbage rolls

1 large onion, diced

2 cloves garlic, minced

1/4 cup (60 mL) butter

1 lb (500 g) fresh brown mushrooms, sliced

1/4 cup (60 mL) chopped fresh thyme

sea salt and freshly ground pepper to taste

1 medium head cabbage

2 cups (500 mL) tomato sauce

1/4 cup (60 mL) heavy cream (32%)

Put rice in a pot with 2 cups (500 mL) vegetable or chicken stock. Bring to a boil, cover and simmer for 10 minutes. Let sit off heat for 10 minutes.

Sauté onion and garlic in butter in a pan. Add mushrooms and cook until liquid has evaporated. Stir in thyme. Add salt and pepper, and adjust to taste.

In a large bowl, combine mushroom mixture with the rice. Set aside.

Cut out core from the cabbage. Bring a large pot of water to a boil and cook cabbage, pulling off leaves as they soften. Drain leaves in a colander or on paper towels. Trim tough stems from cabbage

Other small packets of food from various cuisines now popular in Canada include dolmades and spanikopita (Greek), samosas (Indian), calzones (Italian), cornish pasties (Scottish) spring rolls and wontons (Asian).

leaves and lay the leaves flat on a work surface. Place 1/2 cup (125 mL) filling at base of each leaf, beginning at the thick end of the leaf. Begin rolling at this end, folding edges in as you go to make a neat roll. Place finished cabbage rolls in a casserole dish and cover tightly. Recipe can be completed to this stage up to 24 hours in advance.

Heat tomato sauce in a saucepan. Bring to a boil and add cream. Simmer for 5 minutes and adjust seasoning, if needed.

Preheat oven to 375° F (190° C). Heat the vegetable or chicken stock and pour the hot stock over cabbage rolls just enough to cover them. Bake covered for 25 to 30 minutes until heated through.

Serve with hot tomato sauce and cucumber dill salad.

Silky Chicken Curry

Serves 6

The first immigrants from India were Sikhs who landed in Vancouver in 1904; they found work mostly in the timber industry. Despite institutionalized discrimination that lasted well into that century, Sikhs and other Indians continued to arrive on our shores and contribute to our multicultural landscape. Over the past decade, Indian cuisine has become a major player on the Canadian food scene. Indian restaurants have evolved from obscurity to the point where every major Canadian city has not only a selection of great Indian restaurants but a selection of great *fine dining* Indian restaurants, with flavours and prices that can compete with even the very best French restaurants. This popularity is attributed not only to the character and complexity of the cuisine, which varies regionally within India, but also to Indians being the second-largest Asian ethnic group in Canada, after the Chinese.

1/4 cup (60 mL) unsalted butter

3 medium onions, finely diced

3 cloves garlic, minced

1 Tbsp (15 mL) grated fresh ginger

1/3 cup (75 mL) curry paste

2 tsp (10 mL) freshly ground cumin

pinch of cayenne or chilies (optional)

2 1/2 lbs (1.2 kg) diced chicken or a 4 lb (2 kg) chicken, cut into 10 pieces

2 medium carrots, peeled and diagonally sliced

1 bell pepper, diced

1 medium tomato, diced

1 cup (250 mL) coconut milk

sea salt and freshly ground pepper

fresh cilantro, chopped

1 cup (250 mL) toasted and chopped unsalted cashews

Melt butter over medium heat in a wide, heavy-bottomed pot. Add onions, garlic and ginger and cook about 5 minutes. Stir in curry paste, cumin and cayenne and cook 2 minutes. Add chicken, stirring to coat, then add carrots, pepper, tomato and coconut milk.

Bring to a simmer, cover and cook about 30 minutes, or until chicken is cooked. Season with salt and pepper. Curry can be made up to 3 days in advance and refrigerated.

Serve curry hot, garnished with cilantro and cashews, accompanied by basmati or jasmine rice and a side of plain yogurt or raita (see opposite).

Raita

Peel, seed and grate cucumbers into a colander and let drain 15 minutes. Transfer grated cucumber to a bowl, squeezing out as much moisture as possible, then stir in yogurt, mint, cumin, salt and pepper. Store, refrigerated, for up to 5 days.

Tip

If you don't have an electric rice cooker, try this foolproof method for cooking rice. Cook your rice as you would cook pasta, in a big pot of boiling salted water. Check rice often for doneness, then drain in a fine mesh colander and serve. This method is especially suited to cooking large quantities of rice.

Raita

2 long English cucumbers

1 cup (250 mL) plain yogurt

1/4 cup (60 mL) fresh chopped mint

ground cumin, sea salt and freshly ground pepper to taste

Ginger Beef

Serves 6

In the early to mid-1880s, 17,000 Chinese men came to Canada to build the western section of the Canadian Pacific Railway. They worked in dangerous conditions for half the pay received by white workers, and more than 700 died on the job. After the last spike was driven, these hard-working immigrants were left unemployed and received no assistance from the Canadian government. Using their strong cultural ties to food, many of these men opened restaurants, often along the route of the CPR. The Chinese consider their style of cooking to be a set of methods, not of actual ingredients, so many traditional foods were reinvented using whatever ingredients were available. Ginger beef was invented in Calgary in the mid-1970s by George Wong, owner of the Silver Inn Chinese restaurant. Originally called "deep-fried shredded beef in chili sauce," ginger beef has become a menu fixture of Chinese restaurants nationwide.

1/2 cup (125 mL) water

1 1/2 tsp (7 mL) cornstarch

1/4 cup (60 mL) liquid honey

1 1/2 Tbsp (22 mL) oyster sauce

1/2 tsp (2 mL) dried crushed chilies

2 tsp (10 mL) sesame oil

1/2 cup (125 mL) cornstarch

2 large eggs

1 Tbsp (15 mL) soy sauce

1 tsp (5 mL) sesame oil (optional)

2 cloves garlic, minced or 1/2 tsp (2 mL) powder

1 1/2 tsp (7 mL) finely grated peeled gingerroot

1 1/4 lbs (560 g) sirloin steak, cut across grain into 1/8 inch (3 mm) thick slices

cooking oil, for deep frying

Stir water into first amount of cornstarch in small saucepan. Add next 4 ingredients. Heat, stirring, until boiling and slightly thickened. Remove from heat. Set aside.

Beat next 6 ingredients with fork in medium bowl.

Cut beef slices into 1/4 to 1/2 inch (6 to 12 mm) shreds. Add to egg mixture. Stir until coated. Marinate at room temperature for 15 minutes.

Deep-fry beef, in several batches, in hot (375°F, 190°C) cooking oil for 1 to 1 1/2 minutes, stirring and breaking pieces apart, until golden brown. Remove beef with slotted spoon to paper towels to drain, then transfer to a large bowl. Stir honey mixture. Pour over beef.

Quelque Chose Braised Venison Shanks

Serves 4

The word "venison" comes from the Latin word *venatus,* meaning "chase." Although the term most commonly refers to deer, it also includes meat from moose, elk, caribou and antelope. First Nations peoples historically hunted these animals for food and various other uses, and many Natives carry on these traditions. In the Europe of the Middle Ages, deer hunting was generally reserved for royalty and aristocrats. Woe betide you if you were caught poaching on private hunting grounds: penalties were as severe as blinding and castration. Venison fell out of fashion when fattier alternatives, such as cattle, sheep and hogs, which gave oil for fuel, became widely domesticated. The Disney movie *Bambi,* often called the single most effective anti-hunting propaganda ever, is a more recent reason for the decline in game-animal consumption. Very low in fat and high in protein, venison has drawn renewed interest during the past few diet- and health-crazed years, and a number of deer and elk farms have been set up across the country to meet the demand.

1/4 cup (60 mL) unsalted butter

2 Tbsp (30 mL) olive oil

4 venison shanks, cut osso bucco style by your butcher

sea salt and pepper

2 medium onions, sliced

2 stalks celery, diced

2 carrots, diced

1 head garlic, peeled, cloves left whole

4 star anise, whole

1 stick cinnamon

1 tsp (5 mL) allspice, whole

1 tsp (5 mL) whole black pepper

3 bottles (500 mL size [16 oz]) Quelque Chose cherry beer (see Tip)

1 small handful dried sour cherries

Preheat oven to 350° F (175° C). In a large ovenproof pot or Dutch oven, heat butter and olive oil. Season shanks well with salt and pepper and brown well on all sides. Set aside. Sauté onions in same pot until they begin to caramelize, then add celery, carrots, garlic and spices and sauté until they begin to soften. Pour in beer, scraping pot to loosen any brown bits on bottom. Add cherries and nestle venison shanks into liquid. Cover and braise in oven until meat is very tender, about 2 1/2 hours. Serve with mashed potatoes and a green salad.

Tip

Quelque Chose is a cherry-infused beer that was developed by Québec's Unibroue in 1996 for winter consumption. The brewer recommends warming it to 160° F (70° C) and enjoying it following winter sports. If you have difficulty finding Quelque Chose, substitute a more readily available cherry beer in this recipe.

Osso bucco is a traditional Italian dish using braised veal shanks cut about 1 1/2 inch (3–4 cm) thick. Osso bucco means "hollow bones."

Bison Burger

Serves 4

Hamburgers offer hand-held, on-the-run convenience. Although some form of shaped patties of ground or chopped meat had been consumed in cultures going back at least to the ancient Egyptians, the hamburger really did originate in Hamburg, Germany—sort of. There was no bun, no ketchup and no drive-through; it was just a ground-meat patty known as "Hamburg steak." Several different Americans have claimed credit for inventing the burger as we know it, leading at times to heated controversy, but it is generally agreed that the burger first reached national exposure during the St. Louis World's Fair in 1904. It has never looked back and is now the basis of the fast-food industry. Many combinations of ground meat, bun and condiments have also come and gone, but with the bison burger we have a veritable Canadian rendition.

1 1/2 lbs (750 g) ground bison

1 egg

1 Tbsp (15 mL) grainy Dijon mustard

1/3 cup (75 mL) fine bread crumbs

sea salt and freshly ground pepper

Preheat grill to high. Mix all ingredients together and form into 4 thick patties; thick patties mean juicy burgers, especially when using bison, which is over 85% lean.

Grill patties, turning once, for 4 to 6 minutes per side, until internal temperature reaches 160° F (70° C). Serve patties on toasted buns with your favourite accompaniments.

Tip
For a better burger...

- Handling the meat lightly when mixing and shaping will help prevent it from turning into a hockey puck.

- Make sure the grill is hot to seal in the juices and keep the meat from sticking.

- When shaping your patties, sneak a piece of your favourite cheese (e.g., bleu, Brie or Cheddar) in the centre, making sure it is completely surrounded by the meat, for a volcanic cheeseburger.

Here are some food safety tips when handling raw meat.

- *Store it in the refrigerator and use it within 2 days, or freeze it.*
- *Wash your hands and everything the meat contacted with a solution of 1 tsp unscented bleach per quart of water (5 mL per L).*
- *Do not place the cooked burgers on the same surface the raw meat was on.*
- *Cook ground meat until it reaches a temperature of 160° F (70° C). E. coli is of particular concern for children, the elderly or anyone with a compromised immune system.*

Hawaiian Pizza

Makes 1 12-inch (30 cm) pizza

Pizza as we know it today is a global collaboration. Early Greeks, Egyptians and Romans were all known for using versatile flatbreads and baking them with simple toppings such as olive oil and herbs. In the18th century, these flatbreads made their way to Naples, Italy, and became known as *pizza*. The peasants of the city topped their pizza with water buffalo mozzarella, brought to Italy from Asia. The tomato, once thought poisonous, came from the Americas and was adopted by the Italians as a fundamental ingredient. Pizza has become a worldwide fast-food phenomenon, from deep-dish to New York style and with every topping imaginable, from the delicious to the bizarre. The Hawaiian pizza, a Canadian concoction dating back to 1962 in Chatham, Ontario, is popular across the country.

Crust

1 envelope active dry yeast (1 Tbsp [15 mL])

about 1 1/4 cups (310 mL) warm water, divided

2 cups (500 mL) unbleached, all-purpose flour

1/2 cup (125 mL) whole-wheat flour

1/2 cup (125 mL) cornmeal, plus additional for baking

1 tsp (5 mL) sea salt

1 Tbsp (15 mL) extra virgin olive oil

To activate yeast, dissolve it in 1/4 cup (60 mL) of water and let it sit for about 10 minutes. Combine flours, cornmeal and salt in a bowl. Make a well in centre of flour and pour in yeast, oil and 1 cup (250 mL) water. Stir to combine, adding more water if needed for a soft but not sticky dough.

Turn dough out onto a floured surface and knead until smooth and uniform, about 10 minutes. Divide dough in half, shape into balls and place 1 dough ball seam-side down in an oiled bowl, turning dough over to coat top. (Place remainder in a freezer bag, close tightly and freeze for up to 2 months. Allow to thaw, refrigerated, before use).

Cover bowl with plastic wrap and place in a draft-free spot to rise until doubled, about 1 1/2 hours. Alternatively, dough can be refrigerated up to 24 hours and left to rise at room temperature before using.

Preheat oven to its highest setting, at least 500° F (260° C). If using a pizza stone, preheat it as well. Sprinkle your pizza pan or baking peel (a flat wooden device used to move pizza onto and off pizza stone) with cornmeal.

Remove dough from bowl and flatten. With your hands, pull and stretch dough into a 12-inch (30 cm) circle, taking care not to overwork dough. Place dough on pan or peel, top with sauce and cheese and arrange remaining toppings, adding some cheese to top, if desired. Bake for 12 to 15 minutes or until crust is golden and cheese is bubbling. Serve hot.

Topping

1 cup (250 mL) tomato sauce, canned or homemade

4 oz (125 g) thinly sliced provolone cheese

4 oz (125 g) thinly sliced Parma ham

1 small red onion, thinly sliced

2 cups (500 mL) fresh pineapple chunks

Calzones

For calzones, divide the pizza dough into 6 pieces and roll each into a circle. Place fillings (same as for pizza) in centre of dough and fold dough in half, enclosing fillings. Pinch seam to make a half moon, make a small slit in top to allow steam to escape and bake as for pizza, but for only about 10 minutes.

Cipaille

Serves 8

This traditional layered meat pie is much loved in la belle province. Old British sailor slang calls a "sea pie" a dish of leftovers and vegetables layered into a big pot, and some people believe that cipaille is just the French spelling of this English phrase. Another possible origin for the name of this dish is that it comes from there being six layers to the pie (hence six-pates). The meats used in a cipaille are traditionally game meats such as pheasant and wild boar, but more easily acquired poultry and domesticated meats can be used with great success. The Gaspé region of Québec is famous for its salmon cipaille.

1 lb (500 g) pork, cubed

1 lb (500 g) beef, cubed

4 chicken thighs, boned and cubed

8 oz (250 g) lamb, rabbit or other meat of choice, cubed

2 medium onions, chopped

2 cloves garlic, minced

2 tsp (10 mL) each ground cinnamon, cloves and allspice

8 oz (250 g) thick cut bacon, diced

1 Tbsp (15 mL) sea salt

1 Tbsp (15 mL) freshly ground pepper

3 Tbsp (45 mL) each minced fresh savory and parsley

1 cup (250 mL) red wine

pastry, enough for a double-crust pie (see p. 58 or use purchased)

2 cups (500 mL) mushroom or chicken stock

Combine meats (except bacon), onions, garlic and spices in a bowl and mix well. Cover and refrigerate overnight.

The next morning, preheat oven to 400° F (200° C). Remove meats from fridge. Fry bacon until golden. Mix bacon into bowl of meat and season with salt and pepper. Stir in fresh herbs and wine.

Divide pastry into 4 equal pieces. Roll each out to 1/4 inch (0.5 cm) thickness—they should be slightly larger than container to be used for baking—and cut out a quarter-sized hole from centre of each piece.

Spoon a quarter of meat into an 8-cup (2 L) casserole dish or Dutch oven and top with a pastry layer. Continue layering meat and pastry, ending with a layer of pastry, tucking its edges into sides of casserole dish. Pour 1 cup (250 mL) of stock slowly through hole in pastry. Place casserole dish on a baking sheet to catch drips, and bake for 45 minutes. Turn heat down to 325° F (160° C) and continue to bake for 4 to 5 hours, adding stock through hole as needed to keep casserole moist.

Let sit at least 1/2 hour and up to an hour before serving.

Tip
Note that this recipe needs to be started the evening before serving and requires most of the day to bake.

Another popular addition to cipaille is diced potato. Simply peel and dice 2 large potatoes and add them to the meats.

Humble pie gets its name from the "numbles" (later "umbles," then "humbles") of deer—meat such as the kidney and liver. These parts were stewed with apples, currants, suet and spices, encased in pastry and baked. At one time it was fashionable to eat humble pie, as deer meat was a food reserved for the upper class, but it later became a dish for servants. British settlers brought the recipe to North America, where it was standard fare as late as the 1800s.

Jambon aux Cabane à Sucre

Serves 10 to 12

We have the Native peoples to thank for the springtime tradition of tapping maple trees and gathering their sweet bounty—some North American Natives used maple sugar rather than salt as their basic seasoning. The modern techniques of turning the sap into syrup, sugar and butter were developed and perfected by Canada's French settlers. During the early years, the maple sap offered settlers an income when there was scarce else available to harvest. When demand grew, the man of the house moved deep into the forest, built a cabin and spent the maple season there, gathering and processing the sap. Rare visits from his family at la cabane à sucre were festive events. As the years passed and maple sap production became indus-trialized, the sugar shack tradition has endured with Québeckers and has become a "must" experience for springtime tourists.

3 cups (750 mL) maple syrup

2 cups (500 mL) water

1/4 cup (60 mL) dark rum

3 cups (750 mL) pearl onions

1 x 8 to 10 lb (4 to 6 kg) fully cooked ham, bone in shank end

1 cup (250 mL) maple sugar

1 tsp (5 mL) dry mustard

2 tsp (10 mL) each ground cloves, cumin and coriander

2 Tbsp (30 mL) peppercorns

1/4 cup (60 mL) butter

1/2 cup (125 mL) beef, chicken or vegetable stock

1 cup (250 mL) currants

4 persimmons cut into wedges

Preheat oven to 350° F (175° C). In oven, bring maple syrup and water to a boil in an ovenproof casserole dish large enough for ham. Stir in rum and onions. Place ham in dish, cover and cook for 1 hour.

Meanwhile, to make sauce, combine maple sugar, mustard, spices, butter and stock in a small saucepan and bring to a simmer. Stir in currants. Uncover ham and spoon sauce over ham. Continue to bake for 30 minutes, basting often.

Nestle persimmons into casserole dish and bake for a further 15 minutes. Serve ham warm from oven with sauce.

Tip
Refrigerated, this ham will keep for up to 5 days. It is equally delicious served cold.

La tire ("the pull") is the much-loved climax of any cabane à sucre. To recreate this festive maple treat, boil maple syrup to 238° F (115° C) and pour thinly onto fresh, clean snow. Twirl a popsicle stick in it and enjoy the delicious, sticky taffy.

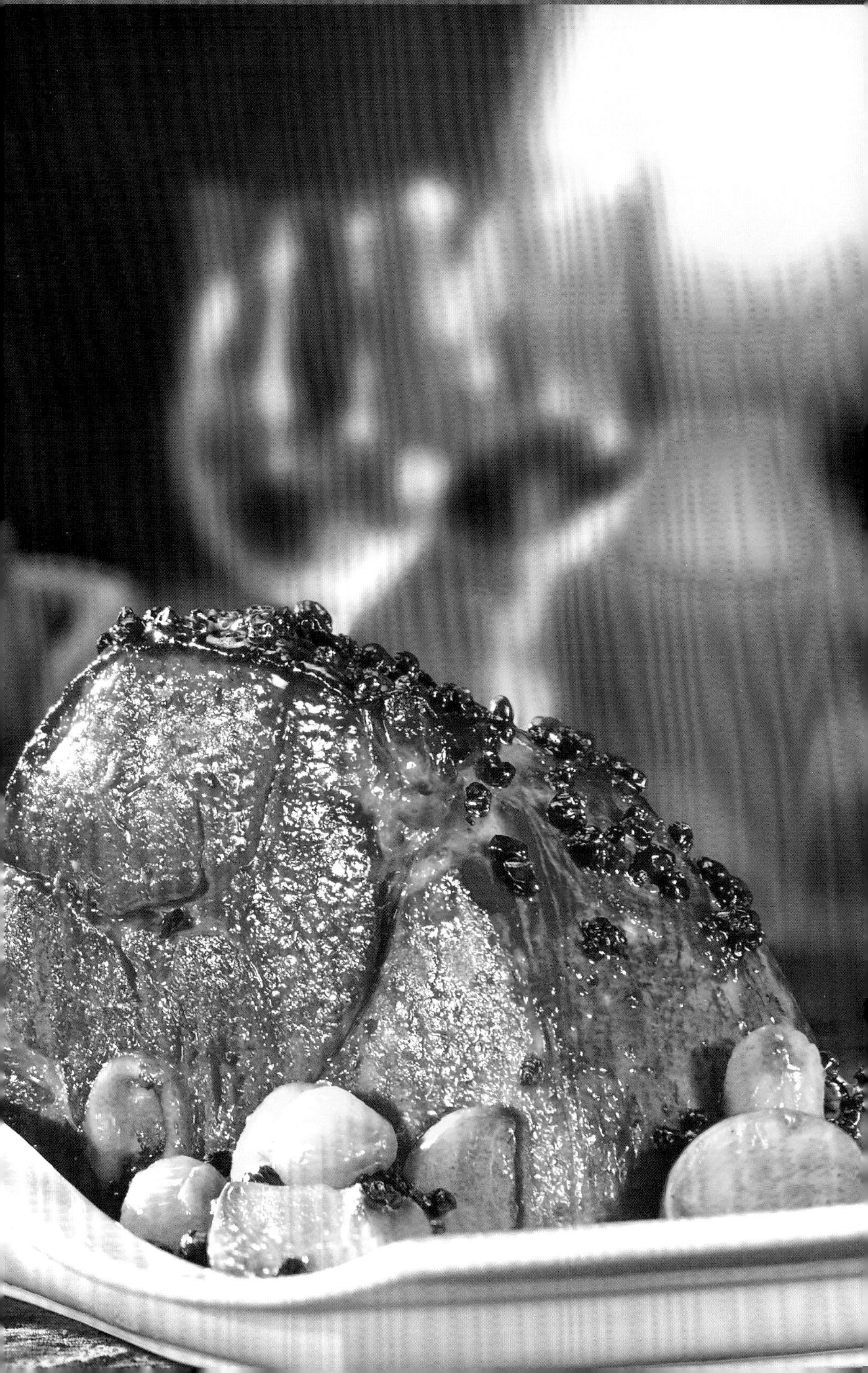

Parmesan-baked Jerusalem Artichokes

Serves 4 to 6

Also known as "sunchoke" and "Canada potato," the Jerusalem artichoke is a tuber native to North America. Its waxy flesh has the texture of a crispy apple and a flavour reminiscent of a sunflower seed. Traditionally, the Jerusalem artichoke was simply boiled and eaten much like a potato, and it can be used in place of potatoes in many recipes. The first written record of this edible member of the sunflower family dates from 1603, when Samuel de Champlain encountered it growing in the vegetable gardens of First Nations peoples. He likened the flavour to that of an artichoke and brought the tuber back to France in 1616. The French initially called it *artichaut de Canada*, and it became a popular vegetable as it made its way through Europe. "Jerusalem" simply comes from the English misunderstanding the Italian word *girasol*, which means "sunflower."

2 lbs (1 kg) Jerusalem artichokes

2 cups (500 mL) heavy cream (32%)

zest and juice of 1 lemon

2 cloves garlic, minced

2 Tbsp (30 mL) chopped fresh thyme

sea salt and freshly cracked pepper

1 cup (250 mL) freshly grated Parmesan

1/2 cup (125 mL) breadcrumbs

olive oil

Preheat oven to 400° F (200° C). Scrub Jerusalem artichokes well, slice 1/8 inch (0.25 cm) thick and put in acidulated water (see below) until needed. In a pot, bring cream, zest and garlic to a boil, remove from heat and let infuse 10 minutes. Stir in lemon juice and thyme and toss with drained Jerusalem artichokes. Season with salt and pepper and bake, covered, in a 9-inch (23 cm) pan for 35 to 40 minutes. Remove from oven.

Set oven to 450° F (230° C). Combine Parmesan and breadcrumbs, then sprinkle evenly overtop artichokes. Drizzle with olive oil. Return to oven for an additional 5 to 7 minutes or until top is golden brown. Let rest 10 minutes before serving.

Acidulated water is just water to which a little acid—normally lemon, lime or vinegar—has been added; 1/2 tsp (2 mL) per cup (250 mL) is enough. When you are peeling or cutting fruits or vegetables that discolour quickly when exposed to air, like apples, place them in acidulated water to prevent browning. Jerusalem artichokes, globe artichokes and salsify are just some of the foods that benefit from this treatment. Acidulated water is also sometimes used for cooking.

Pan-fried Fiddlehead Greens

Serves 4 to 6

Ostrich fern (*Matteuccia struthiopteris*) grows across the country in moist or wet forested areas, but the consumption of fiddleheads is most strongly associated with New Brunswick; up to 23,000 kilograms are gathered there annually. Long harvested by the Mi'kmaq and Maliseet peoples of eastern Canada, this seasonal treat is appreciated equally for the joy of the harvest as for the taste. These First Nations people were, and still are, crazy about this little fern, which they consider a delicacy. They believe it has a cleansing quality, a sort of rejuvenation after the long winter months. Even today, it is referred to as the first fruit of the season, the first of nature's offerings to peek through the soil after the long, cold winter. Luckily, given that the wild harvest is only a short three weeks and the best growing spots are carefully guarded family secrets, we can find fiddleheads in some grocery stores— including several brands of frozen ones—and at local farmers' markets. Watch your sources carefully in spring for this unusual fern to make its appearance.

1 lb (500 g) fresh fiddleheads

1/3 cup (75 mL) unsalted butter

juice of 1/2 lemon

pinch each of sea salt, pepper, paprika

1/3 cup (75 mL) fine breadcrumbs

Clean fiddleheads well and cook in boiling, salted water for 5 to 7 minutes. In a pan, melt butter and add lemon juice, salt, pepper, paprika and breadcrumbs. Toss hot fiddleheads in pan to coat well. Serves 6 as a side dish.

Tip
A great way to clean the papery, brown scales from fiddleheads is to shake them in small batches in a paper bag.

Traditional Steamed New Brunswick Fiddlehead Greens

Prepare fiddleheads by washing them well in several changes of clean water, then steam until tender, about 10 minutes. While still hot, toss with butter and vinegar. Season with salt and pepper.

Traditional Steamed New Brunswick Fiddlehead Greens

1 lb (500 g) fresh fiddleheads

1/4 cup (60 mL) unsalted butter

2 Tbsp (30 mL) champagne vinegar or cider vinegar

sea salt and pepper to taste

Creamed Spinach with Butter Beans

Serves 6 to 8

Spinach, along with kale and wild blueberries, is now known as a top-rated source of health-giving antioxidants. Believed to have first been cultivated in Persia over 2000 years ago, this vegetable is still sometimes referred to as "Persian green." In the 12th century, the Moors introduced spinach to Spain, and it began to make its way through the rest of Europe. Catherine de Medici of Florence was so fond of spinach that, when she married the King of France, she brought with her personal chefs who knew how to prepare this jade-coloured green just the way she liked it. Since then, dishes enriched with spinach have become known as "à la Florentine." Spinach grows best in cool climates, which makes it particularly well suited to much of Canada, and it is a popular crop for home gardeners.

3 lbs (1.5 kg) fresh baby spinach

1 Tbsp (15 mL) unsalted butter, plus 1/3 cup (75 mL)

1 small onion, diced

1 cup (250 mL) fresh shiitake mushrooms, stemmed and thinly sliced (or reconstitute half the volume of dried ones)

salt and pepper to taste

1 garlic clove, minced

1/3 cup (75 mL) flour

2 cups (500 mL) whole milk

pinch of freshly grated nutmeg

1 can (340 mL) butter beans (lima beans), drained and rinsed

Steam spinach until just wilted; let it cool and squeeze out as much liquid as possible. Chop coarsely.

Melt 1 Tbsp (15 mL) of butter over medium-high heat until foamy. Add onion and sauté until starting to caramelize, then add mushrooms. Season with salt and pepper, and cook mushrooms for about 5 minutes or until they have released all their moisture. Remove from heat and stir in garlic.

In a heavy saucepan, melt 1/3 cup (75 mL) of butter. Stir in flour and cook over low heat for 5 minutes. Scald milk in a separate pan and pour into butter and flour, stirring and cooking for 10 minutes until you have a smooth, thick sauce. Season with nutmeg, salt and pepper. Stir in spinach, beans and mushroom mixture. Cook until heated through, and serve hot.

Tip
This dish works well with almost any bean; black beans or cranberry beans offer a stunning contrast of colour. You can also pour the creamed spinach (with or without the beans and mushrooms) into a buttered casserole dish, top with grated Gruyère or Cheddar cheese and bake at 375° F (190° C) until golden. This alternative works very well for reheating leftovers the following day.

Scalloped Potatoes

Serves 6 to 8

The potato, a native of the high Andes and first cultivated as long as 10,000 years ago, was transformed into *gratin dauphinois* in the Dauphiné region of the French Alps, where the evolution of potato dishes benefited from the cold weather. The potatoes were sliced and layered with cream, using much the same method as was the custom for preparing scallops—hence the English name for the dish. Nowadays in Canada, we love to use the Yukon Gold potato, which was developed by potato breeder Gary Johnston during the 1960s at the University of Guelph. The first Canadian potato to be sold by name and a perfect match to cold-weather potato dishes, it has become a favourite for its texture, flavour and tempting, golden flesh.

1 1/2 cups (375 mL) freshly grated Gruyère cheese

1/2 cup (125 mL) freshly grated Parmesan cheese

1 medium onion, diced

1 Tbsp (15 mL) butter

2 cloves garlic, minced

2 cups (500 mL) heavy cream (32%)

1 tsp (5 mL) freshly grated nutmeg

4 lbs (2 kg) Yukon Gold potatoes, peeled and thinly sliced

sea salt and freshly ground pepper

1/4 cup (60 mL) chopped fresh thyme

Preheat oven to 350° F (175° C). Combine Gruyère and Parmesan and put aside. Sauté onion in butter until soft. Add garlic and cook for 2 minutes. Add cream, bring just to a boil and remove from heat. Stir in nutmeg. Butter an 8-cup (2 L) shallow baking dish. Layer potato slices in baking dish, season each layer with salt, pepper and thyme and add a sprinkle of cheeses. Continue layering until potatoes are all used, then pour cream sauce overtop. Top with remaining cheese, cover and bake for 35 to 40 minutes or until you can easily pierce centre of potatoes with a knife. Remove cover and continue cooking until top is golden brown, about 10 more minutes. Let rest at least 10 minutes and up to 1/2 hour before serving.

Finnan Haddie Gratin

The traditional Scottish smoked fish, finnan haddie gets its name from the Aberdeen village of Findon (pronounced Finnan) where the residents first began to produce a tastier version of smoked haddock (haddie) in the 19th century. This fish has remained popular in the Maritimes for hundreds of years, and it pairs well with scalloped potatoes. To make your scalloped potatoes into a finnan haddie gratin, simply shred 8 oz (250 g) of smoked haddock with your fingers and add some to each layer of the recipe. Cook as directed and enjoy.

Poutine

Serves 8

A beloved staple of Québec cuisine, poutine is served at fast-food restaurants and fine dining establishments alike. Popular variations replace the gravy with Bolognese sauce or add sausages, and Montréal's famous Au Pied de Cochon serves its poutine with foie gras! There are many stories about the origin of poutine, but the consensus is that it originated in rural Québec in the 1950s. Ultra-fresh cheese curds are the key ingredient in authentic poutine. They must be fresh enough to become soft (but not melt) once nestled in amongst the hot fries and gravy. A great indication of their freshness is how they squeak between your teeth when you chew them. The very popular fry-making method described below produces excellent, crisp fries with a creamy interior. It is a little extra work because it requires "blanching" the potatoes in oil at a low temperature to cook them, then frying them again at high temperature to brown them, but it is worth the effort if you are going to indulge anyway.

8 cups (2 L) veal or beef stock	To make gravy, place stock in a pan, bring to a boil and simmer, roughly 1 hour, until reduced to a glaze.
oil for deep frying	
8 medium russet potatoes	In a fryer or large pot, heat oil to 325° F (160° C). Wash and dry potatoes (peel if desired) and cut them into fries. Fry potatoes in 2 batches for about 5 minutes, or until they are cooked but still pale. Transfer them to a perforated pan or paper towels to drain and cool; they can be left for up to 1 hour.
4 gourmet sausages, such as chorizo or merguez (North African)	
2 cups (500 mL) fresh cheese curds	
sea salt and freshly ground pepper	Grill sausages and set aside.
	Bring cheese to room temperature. Just before serving, heat oil to 375° F (190° C). Reheat sausage and gravy.

Re-fry cooled potatoes in oil until golden and crisp. Drain quickly on paper towel and season with salt and pepper. Transfer fries to individual bowls or ramekin dishes. (Parchment cones, as pictured, make this dish "portable"—great for backyard barbecues!) Slice sausage and divide amongst bowls. Top with cheese and gravy. Serve immediately.

Oven-baked Fries

Oven baking reduces oil content of fries. Preheat oven to 475° F (245° C). Prepare potatoes as in main recipe and place in a large bowl. Toss with 1/4 cup (60 mL) olive oil, sea salt, paprika and freshly ground pepper to taste—experiment by adding your favourite herbs and spices, flavoured oils, etc. Bake for 20 to 25 minutes, turning once, or until potatoes are cooked and crispy. Once cool, fries can be refrigerated for up to 2 days and reheated in a 400° F (200° C) oven for about 8 minutes.

Wild Mushroom Pierogi

Serves 8 to 10

Depending on the ethnic context, dough pockets with a filling might be called *pyrohy, varenyky, pilmeni, ravioli, kreplach, wontons* or *gyozas. Pierogi* (pyrohy) originated in Poland following the second marriage of King Zygmunt (Sigismund I) of Poland in 1517 to Bona Sforza, a princess from Milan who brought chefs from Italy and France to rejuvenate Polish cuisine. From Poland, pierogi made their way through Central and Eastern Europe, with fillings such as potato, cheese, sauerkraut, meat or various fruits. Pierogi arrived in Canada during the mid-1800s with the first wave of Polish immigrants, but their popularity on the Prairies must be attributed to the Ukrainian immigrants who settled the aspen parkland stretching from Manitoba to Alberta around the end of the 19th century. Although pierogi are not difficult to make, they are time consuming. This twist on the classic recipe has a wild mushroom filling.

Filling

2 Tbsp (30 mL) butter

3 cups (750 mL) chopped wild mushrooms

1/3 cup (75 mL) finely chopped yellow onion

1 egg yolk

1 Tbsp (15 mL) chopped fresh dill

salt and freshly ground pepper

Dough

4 1/2 cups (1.1 L) all-purpose flour

2 tsp (10 mL) salt

2 Tbsp (30 mL) butter, melted

2 cups (500 mL) sour cream

2 eggs

1 egg yolk

2 Tbsp (30 mL) olive oil

Melt butter in large sauté pan over medium heat. Add mushrooms and onion. Cook, stirring, until mushrooms are tender and liquid has evaporated, about 7 to 9 minutes. Remove from heat. Add egg yolk and dill, and season to taste with salt and pepper. Stir to combine. Set aside.

Stir together flour and salt in large bowl. In second bowl, combine butter, sour cream, eggs, egg yolk and oil. Add wet ingredients to dry. Stir until well combined. Cover with damp kitchen towel and let stand 15 to 20 minutes.

To assemble, divide dough into 3 roughly equal portions. On lightly floured work surface, roll out 1 portion of dough to 1/16 inch (2 mm) thick. Keep remaining dough covered. Use a 3 inch (7.5 cm) round cutter to cut as many rounds in dough as will fit. Place 1 tsp (5 mL) filling on one half of each round. Lightly moisten the other half of each round with water. Fold over other half. Lightly pinch edges together to seal. Transfer to cloth-lined baking sheet.

Repeat with remaining dough and filling. Leftover dough may be re-rolled once. (Pierogies may be made up to this point then frozen on baking sheets before transferring to freezer bags to keep for up to 1 month.)

To cook, bring large pot of salted water to boil over medium-high heat. Cook pierogies, in batches, stirring gently to prevent sticking, until they float to the surface, about 1 to 2 minutes. Use a slotted spoon to transfer to colander to drain.

Melt butter in large sauté pan over medium heat. Add onion. Cook, stirring, until softened and almost golden, about 5 minutes. Add pierogies. Stir to coat and warm through. Serve warm with sour cream.

Topping

2 Tbsp (30 mL) butter

1 medium onion, diced

sour cream

Molasses and Rum Baked Beans

Serves 6

Beans! Our settlers relied on them, our explorers and fur trappers regarded them as a necessity, our armies consumed them in large quantities, and, during the Klondike Gold Rush, they sold for $1.50 per pound. Because they complement grains to supply all the required amino acids, beans and other legumes have been vital in the diet of cultures around the world. The first known legume cultivation dates back to 9750 BC, in Thailand. Long before European explorers came to North America, the Iroquois and other Native North Americans were making baked beans, combining the beans with maple syrup and bear fat in earthenware pots that were baked in hot coals. The settlers learned this cooking method from the Natives, substituting molasses and pork fat. Although not used nearly as much today, molasses (treacle to the British) was a cheap, convenient and ubiquitous sweetener before improved methods of sugar refinement reduced sugar prices following World War I.

1 lb (500 g) dried navy beans

2 tsp (10 mL) olive oil

1 clove garlic, minced

3 bay leaves

1 cup (250 mL) finely diced onion

2 tsp (10 mL) Worcestershire sauce

1/4 cup (60 mL) dark brown sugar

1/2 cup (125 mL) unsulphured molasses

1/4 cup (60 mL) ketchup

1 Tbsp (15 mL) apple cider or balsamic vinegar

1 Tbsp (15 mL) Dijon mustard

1 Tbsp (15 mL) tamari

1/2 cup (125 mL) dark rum

3 cups (750 mL) hot water, plus additional as needed

Place beans in a large pot of boiling water over high heat. Once water has returned to a boil, turn off heat and let stand 1 hour.

Preheat oven to 275° F (135° C). Drain beans and place in a large mixing bowl. Add remaining ingredients, except water, and mix well.

Brush 8-cup (2 L) Dutch oven or ovenproof bean pot with olive oil, add bean mixture and pour hot water overtop. Bake, covered, for 5 to 7 hours or until beans are tender, gently stirring in additional water as liquid is absorbed by beans.

Tip
This dish needs to bake for more than 5 hours, so get an early start!

Maple Baked Beans

Follow recipe for Molasses and Rum-baked Beans, omitting sugar, Worcestershire sauce, half of molasses and tamari. Add 1 cup (250 mL) maple syrup and 1 cup (250 mL) diced salt pork.

Herbed Colcannon

Serves 6 to 8

It is said that the potato first reached Ireland in 1588, washed up on Irish shores from the wreckage of ships in the Spanish Armada. The first Europeans to really embrace this tuber, the Irish came to depend on it for both food and security. The potato crops started to fail in the early 1800s, and by 1846, the Irish were suffering a full-fledged famine. Almost two million Irish—40% of the population—fled Ireland or were sent abroad, with hundreds of thousands coming to Canada. With them came *boxty, champ, colcannon* and many other wonderful potato dishes. Colcannon has changed over the years from a simple mash of cabbage and potatoes to a boiled hash of as many as eight vegetables, white ones being preferred. Typically enjoyed on All Hallows' Eve, traditional colcannon was served with hidden trinkets to tell the future; discovering a ring meant marriage, whereas a thimble or button meant celibacy.

2 medium rutabagas, peeled and cubed

2 parsnips, peeled and cubed

3 medium potatoes, peeled and cubed

1 medium onion, sliced

1/2 cup (125 mL) butter, divided

water or light vegetable stock, as needed

1/2 cup (125 mL) sour cream

1 Tbsp (15 mL) minced fresh thyme

1 egg, lightly beaten

sea salt and freshly ground pepper

1 package Boursin cheese, any savoury flavour (see below)

2/3 cup (150 mL) chopped fresh parsley

Combine all vegetables in a saucepan with 1 Tbsp (15 mL) of butter. Cover with water or light vegetable stock, and simmer 10 to 15 minutes or until tender. Drain, reserving enough liquid to make a smooth purée when cooked vegetables have been mashed. Fold in remaining ingredients, reserving some parsley for garnish.

Boursin is a brand of cheese developed in Gournay, France, with a texture reminiscent of fluffy cream cheese. It is available in most grocery stores and is well worth seeking out for its variety of great flavours. In a pinch, you could use 4–5 oz (125–140 g) regular cream cheese.

Succotash

Serves 4 to 6

Succotash in its most basic form pairs two First Nations staples: corn and beans. European settlers adapted it to their tastes by adding butter, seasoning and a bit of salt pork. Many variations exist, with many types of beans used. We've used soybeans and added some more of nature's bounty to round out the dish: mushrooms, peppers and spinach. If you have semi-repressed memories of succotash as a mess of overcooked, mushy vegetables, our freshly made version will be a happy surprise.

2 slices bacon, cut crosswise into very thin strips

1 Tbsp (15 mL) butter

2 cups (500 mL) fresh corn kernels (from 3 to 4 ears)

2 cups (500 mL) shelled edamame

1 cup (250 mL) sliced or torn fresh mushrooms (use whatever is available)

1/2 cup (125 mL) diced red bell pepper

3/4 cup (175 mL) whipping cream (30 percent)

1/4 cup (60 mL) water

1/2 tsp (2 mL) each salt and freshly ground black pepper

2 cups (500 mL) baby spinach leaves

1 bunch of green onions, thinly sliced

Cook bacon in heavy skillet over medium heat, stirring frequently, until crisp, about 5 minutes. Transfer bacon with slotted spoon to paper towels to drain, then add butter to bacon fat in skillet and melt. Add corn, edamame, mushrooms and red pepper, and cook, stirring, for 2 minutes. Add cream, water, salt and pepper, then simmer, partially covered, until vegetables are tender, 10 to 15 minutes. Stir in bacon, spinach and green onions. Cook until spinach begins to wilt. Season to taste with salt and pepper. Serve immediately.

Yam Latkes

Makes 12 latkes

We have our Jewish population to thank for bagels with lox, Montréal smoked meats and latkes. Canada's first Jews arrived in the 1760s and settled in Québec. Russia's pogroms of the late 1800s and subsequent anti-Semitism in Eastern Europe sent more Jews to our shores; they were later joined by Holocaust survivors and North African Jews. About 350,000 Jewish people now live in Canada, with nearly half of them residing in Toronto and another quarter in Montréal. Potato pancakes originated in the Slavic nations and were adopted by the large Jewish communities who lived there; the word *latke* is of Russian origin. The oil used to fry these traditional pancakes—an integral part of the Hanukkah celebration—celebrates the miracle of Hanukkah oil. When the Maccabees defeated the Syrian army in 165 BC and reclaimed the Temple of Jerusalem, they found only enough oil to light their menorah (the Jewish candelabra) for one night, but it miraculously burned for eight.

2 lbs (1 kg) yams, such as garnet yams, peeled

1 yellow onion, peeled

1 egg, beaten

2 Tbsp (30 mL) flour

1/4 cup (60 mL) fresh herbs (dill, thyme, rosemary—whatever is on hand)

sea salt and pepper

oil for frying

Grate yams in batches. Squeeze out as much liquid as possible; this step is vital for crispy latkes (bundling in cheesecloth works well). Place yams in a large bowl and grate in onion. Stir in egg, then add flour and herbs. Season with salt and pepper. Heat oil in a large skillet and fry each latke until crisp and golden, turning once. You can make latkes as small or large as you like. Serve with sour cream, mushroom gravy or applesauce.

Tip
You can jazz up latkes by grating in vegetables such as carrots or parsnips or adding garlic or even grated apple; just be sure to keep the bulk of your mixture starchy. To make a more traditional latke, use russet potatoes. For a different texture, try a finer or coarser grater.

Poutine Râpée

A similar preparation for potatoes, called kartoffel kloesse, *came to Canada by way of German settlers. New Brunswick Acadians adopted it as* poutine râpée.

Bring a large pot of salted water to a boil. Squeeze out as much liquid as possible from grated potatoes and combine potatoes with remaining ingredients. Form into plum-sized dumplings (if using pork, push a cube into centre of each dumpling, enclosing potato mixture around it). Drop into boiling water and cook until done, about 15 minutes. Serve with a savoury gravy or sugar and molasses.

Poutine Râpée

3 cups (750 mL) grated Yukon Gold potatoes

2/3 cup (150 mL) mashed potato

1/4 cup (60 mL) flour

1 tsp (5 mL) sea salt

1 egg, beaten

salt pork, diced (optional)

Vanilla and Poppy Seed French Toast

Serves 4

What we call French toast has different names elsewhere; in England, for example, it is called "poor knights of Windsor," after a military order founded in the 14th century. French toast apparently originated in Ancient Rome, where it was made with the finest bread—frequently paired with costly spices and almond milk—as a treat for the well-to-do. In France, this recipe acquired the name *pain perdu* ("lost bread") after it became a popular method for using stale bread, and French immigrants likely brought it with them to our country. During the frugal times, French toast was much appreciated by Canada's pioneers as a way to use up scraps of bread and keep bellies full. In Québec, it is now usually found on the menu as *pain doré* ("golden bread"). Savoury versions of French toast are often served with ketchup.

4 eggs, beaten

1/4 cup (60 mL) milk

1/4 cup (60 mL) heavy cream (32%)

1/2 vanilla bean, seed scrapings only (see p. 32)

pinch of sea salt

1 cup (250 mL) spelt or kamut flakes

1/2 cup (125 mL) poppy seeds

3 Tbsp (45 mL) brown sugar

1 tsp (5 mL) cinnamon

1/8 tsp (0.5 mL) cardamom

unsalted butter for frying

8 slices fairly stale bread

fresh berries and maple syrup for serving

Whisk together eggs, milk, cream, vanilla and salt until frothy. In a separate bowl, mix together spelt or kamut flakes, poppy seeds, brown sugar, cinnamon and cardamom. Place a nonstick skillet with a dab of butter on medium heat. Dip a bread slice in egg mixture, allowing it to soak up a bit of liquid, then dredge in flake mixture. Fry until golden. Repeat with remaining slices and serve with berries and maple syrup.

Vanilla beans are pricey, so it is a good idea to get the most of out of what you buy. After using the bean in your recipe, rinse the pod, let it dry and place it in your sugar jar to infuse the sugar with the beautiful vanilla flavour. You could, alternatively, soak the pods in your jug of maple syrup or even a bottle of vodka and let the vanilla do its magic. Allow at least a few days for soaking; the longer you allow the vanilla to infuse, the stronger the flavour will be.

Flavoured Bannock

Serves 4

Because of bannock's ease of preparation and versatility, this traditional Scottish quick bread was important to Canada's early settlers and fur traders. Every year at the winter carnivals in northern Manitoba, such as those in Flin Flon and The Pas, trappers still compete in bannock-baking contests. This bread also became popular with Canada's First Nations. Natives had been making quick breads—called *pakwejigan* in a number of their languages—for many hundreds of years with available ingredients such as corn. However, once European settlers introduced them to bannock and wheat flour became readily available, the Natives adopted the new recipe so enthusiastically that it has become integral to First Nations cuisines across the country.

1 1/4 cups (310 mL) flour

1 Tbsp (15 mL) baking powder

1 tsp (5 mL) sea salt

1 Tbsp (15 mL) sugar

3 Tbsp (45 mL) butter

1 egg

about 1/2 cup (125 mL) water

a handful or combination of any of the following: chopped nuts, banana chips, dried fruit, cheese, cinnamon sugar, chocolate chips, seeds, fresh berries or whatever else you can come up with

oil for cooking

Combine flour, baking powder, salt and sugar. Rub butter into flour mixture. Combine egg and some of the water and add to flour mixture, stirring to combine. Add enough water to make a firm dough. Knead dough (adding optional ingredients if desired) for about 3 minutes. Let dough rest, covered, for 30 minutes. Divide dough into quarters and shape each portion into a ball, then flatten with a rolling pin or your hand into a disk about 1/2 inch (12 mm) thick. Heat a frying pan over medium heat and add 1 Tbsp (15 mL) oil. Cook bannock on both sides, turning once, until golden brown. Add more oil as necessary.

Tip
You can prepare the dough up to 24 hours in advance; wrap tightly and refrigerate. It can be fried or baked, or when camping, you can forego the frying pan and simply twist the dough evenly around a clean stick and hold over an open campfire until golden and crispy.

Crêpes

Makes 35 to 40 crêpes

Crêpes originated in Brittany, but they can be found in many other cuisines. In Hungary, they are known as *palacsinta,* in Italy as *crespelle* and in Russia as *blinchiki,* but they are always paper thin and made with an egg-based batter. How crêpes are folded and the filling they contain reflect the local customs and traditions of the countries in which they are served. They are sometimes even cut into thin strips and served like a fresh pasta in soups. This versatility was best described by a Polish chef who said that *nalesniki* are like envelopes—you can fill them with anything. In France, it is customary to make a wish holding a coin while touching the handle of the crêpe pan and turning the crêpe, although we recommend a great deal of crêpe-making practice before attempting this trick! Crêperies are now found pretty well across Canada, with two of the most renowned ones in Québec City and Montréal.

2 cups (500 mL) all-purpose flour **1/2 tsp (2 mL) sea salt** **12 whole eggs, lightly beaten**	Sift flour and salt into a large bowl. Add eggs and start whisking. Gradually add milk, whisking continuously to make a smooth batter. Whisk in oil, cover and refrigerate for 15 minutes. Whisk again and refrigerate for up to 24 hours, until ready to use.
3 cups (750 mL) whole milk **1/3 cup (75 mL) vegetable oil, plus additional for cooking**	Preheat a crêpe pan over medium-high heat and pour batter into it, swirling to coat bottom; for a 9-inch (23 cm) crêpe pan, use about 1/4 cup (60 mL) of batter. Cook until barely browned, turn and cook an additional 10 seconds.

Transfer crêpe to a plate and continue cooking remaining batter, stacking cooked crêpes on top of each other. Add filling as desired, fold and serve.

Tip
For easiest cooking, use an authentic crêpe pan rather than a regular skillet.

Crêpes can be covered with plastic wrap and refrigerated for up to 2 days. To freeze for up to 3 months, separate with parchment paper and wrap well in plastic wrap; thaw in the fridge before use. To refresh crêpes, warm in a low oven (200° F [90° C]) for about 1 minute.

Crêpes can be filled with fresh fruit and served with maple syrup and whipped cream. They also work well with savoury fillings, such as mushrooms in a cream sauce or chicken with spinach and feta cheese. The crêpes pictured were filled with cottage cheese, raisins and orange zest, then dusted with icing sugar.

Sourdough Hotcakes

Makes about 1 dozen

The first leavened breads rose through the action of yeast naturally occurring on the grains and in the air. Before the advent of modern yeast packaging methods, people wanting to bake bread would keep a "starter" containing a proven yeast strain. Prospectors in the San Francisco Gold Rush discovered that their starters were unusually tangy, and the term "sourdough" was born. The name was soon applied to the prospectors themselves, and they brought both their starters and the name along to subsequent gold rushes in Canada. The conditions of the Klondike were so harsh that the North-West Mounted Police would not allow anyone over the Chilkoot Pass without a year's worth of provisions. Because it could breathe life into the most meagre supplies during a time when food was even more important than money, sourdough was extremely valuable to these prospectors, and it is still popular as a leavening agent today.

Quick Sourdough Starter

1 cup (250 mL) water

1 cup (250 mL) unbleached flour

1/2 tsp (2 mL) active dry yeast

Sourdough Hotcakes

2 cups (500 mL) sourdough starter (see above)

1 1/2 cups (375 mL) unbleached or whole-wheat flour

2 Tbsp (30 mL) sugar, maple syrup or honey

3 Tbsp (45 mL) oil

2 eggs

1/2 tsp (2 mL) sea salt

1 tsp (5 mL) baking powder

1 tsp (5 mL) baking soda, diluted in 1 Tbsp (15 mL) warm water

The night before you plan to make hotcakes, mix starter ingredients well and set out on a countertop in a draft-free area, allowing starter time to develop its characteristic sour taste. Remaining starter can be left on the counter for future use; it is best stored at 65 to 77° F (18 to 25° C). To strengthen and "feed" starter, add 1/4 cup (60 mL) water and 1/4 cup (60 mL) flour every second day.

Preheat griddle or pan to medium-high heat. Mix hotcake ingredients, except soda, together. Gently fold in soda and cook cakes right away so as to not lose soda's leavening effect. Serve hot with your favourite condiments.

Old-fashioned Sourdough Starter

Boil unpeeled potatoes until they fall apart. Remove skins. Mash potatoes in a nonmetallic bowl, adding water as needed to make a rich, thick liquid, about 2 cups (500 mL). Add remaining ingredients, beating until smooth, and let stand for 1 week. Feed starter as described for quick starter.

Old-fashioned Sourdough Starter

2 large potatoes

3 Tbsp (45 mL) sugar

1 2/3 cups (400 mL) unbleached flour

1/2 tsp (2 mL) active dry yeast

Icelandic Brown Bread

Makes 2 loaves

The Iceland Festival, which is celebrated on August 2 by Canadian Icelanders, marks the occasion when Icelandic immigrants first established a colony at Gimli, Manitoba, in 1875. Between 1870 and 1900, 25% of Icelanders left their country for the promise of a better life, many of them choosing "New Iceland" in Manitoba because of the availability of land and the similarity in climate. Canada now boasts the only community of ethnic Icelanders outside Iceland who primarily speak their native language and who have held fast to their many traditions, including this dense, healthy and flavourful bread.

2 Tbsp (30 mL) active dry yeast

1/4 cup (60 mL) warm water

2 1/2 cups (625 mL) very warm water

1/4 cup (60 mL) honey

1/2 cup (125 mL) cold-pressed canola oil

1/2 cup (125 mL) blackstrap molasses

3 cups (750 mL) whole-wheat flour

3 cups (750 mL) unbleached flour, plus additional to achieve proper consistency

2 tsp (10 mL) sea salt

1 1/2 cups (375 mL) mix of your favourite nuts and seeds, such as flax, sesame, sunflower, oatmeal, oat bran or ground or chopped nuts

In a small bowl, activate yeast with 1/4 cup (60 mL) water and set aside for 5 to 10 minutes. In a separate bowl, mix together rest of water, honey, oil and molasses. In a third bowl, combine flours and salt.

Add yeast water to liquid ingredients and begin to stir in flour mixture 1 cup (250 mL) at a time. Add in nuts and seeds with last cup of flour. Turn dough out onto a lightly floured surface and knead for about 10 minutes, adding more flour to make it smooth. Place dough in an oiled bowl, cover, set in a draft-free location and let rise until doubled, roughly 1 hour.

Punch dough down and let rise again, until doubled, about 20–30 minutes. Divide dough in half, place into 2 lightly oiled 1 1/2 pound (1.5 L) loaf pans, cover and let rise until each loaf rises to edge of pan. Meanwhile, preheat oven to 400° F (200° C). Bake for 15 minutes, then turn down heat and continue baking at 350° F (175° C) until done, about 40 minutes.

Tip

As with all yeast breads, rising times will vary depending on room temperature and humidity.

This bread will stay fresh for 4 days if kept in an airtight container. It also freezes well for up to 3 months.

Pulla

Makes 1 loaf

The earliest Finns to immigrate to Canada made their way to southern B.C. via Alaska in the 1800s. Like the Chinese, the Finns are famed for their work on the Canadian Pacific Railway, and they also found employment in the timber trade, in Ontario's mines and on the construction of the Welland Canal. Today, Thunder Bay boasts one of the largest Finnish communities outside of Finland. Finns here and in Finland consume more coffee per capita than almost any other nationality. The sweet coffee bread known as *pulla* is a popular Finnish recipe, as are the orange-flavoured *mammi* Easter pudding, a wide range of savoury and sweet pies, a fish soup called *mojakka* and, of course, rye bread.

3/4 cup (175 mL) 2% milk

1/2 cup (125 mL) brown sugar

1/3 cup (75 mL) butter

1 envelope (1 Tbsp [15 mL]) active dry yeast

1 tsp (5 mL) sugar

1/4 cup (60 mL) warm water

2 eggs, beaten

1/2 tsp (2 mL) ground cardamom

1 tsp (5 mL) sea salt

1 cup (250 mL) whole-wheat flour

2 cups (500 mL) unbleached flour, plus up to 2 cups (500 mL) more

1 Tbsp (15 mL) coffee

1 Tbsp (15 mL) milk

1 egg, beaten

1/3 cup (75 mL) unbleached sugar

Scald milk in a pot; remove from heat and stir in brown sugar and butter. Let mixture cool to lukewarm.

Dissolve yeast and sugar in warm water and let stand 5 to 10 minutes to activate yeast.

Once milk mixture is cool, stir in 2 eggs, cardamom, yeast mixture and salt. Beat in whole-wheat flour and 1 cup (250 mL) of unbleached flour. Continue adding flour, 1/2 cup (125 mL) at a time, until you have medium-firm dough. Dust a work surface and knead dough for 10 minutes, adding flour if dough is sticky.

Lightly oil a large bowl and set dough inside, turning once to coat top. Cover with plastic wrap and a towel (to hold in some heat) and let rise until doubled, about 1 1/2 hours.

Punch down, and divide dough into thirds. Roll each piece into a strand 18 inches (45 cm) long. Braid strands into a loaf and place on an oiled baking sheet. Let rise, covered, until almost doubled, about 40 minutes.

Preheat oven to 375° F (190° C). Combine coffee, milk and egg in a bowl. Once pulla is ready to bake, brush this liquid on as a glaze and sprinkle with sugar. Bake for 30 to 35 minutes or until golden and bread springs back when pressed firmly.

Tip
This bread is best when served the same day, and it is even more delicious served warm; be sure to allow for the rising and baking times when scheduling the serving time for oven-fresh pulla. Day-old pulla is excellent for toast, bread pudding and French toast.

Montréal-style Bagels

Makes 12 bagels

Along with smoked meat—the specialty of Schwartz's, Dunn's and Lester's delicatessens—Montréal is known for its bagels. The history of the bagel in Canada is a bit murky, but it is commonly accepted that Jewish settlers from Poland (or eastern Europe) brought it to North America around 1880. Two men are named as the potential father of the Montreal bagel: Isadore Shlafman and Chaim Seligman. Shlafman opened the Fairmount, Montréal's first bagel bakery, in 1919, but both men were selling their wares from street carts long before that. Seligman, along with Myer Lewkowicz, opened St-Viateur Bagel in 1957, and the two establishments have been vying for supremacy ever since. Both use wood-fired ovens to produce an extra crispy outside while maintaining a melt-in-your-mouth centre.

1 envelope (1 Tbsp [15 mL]) active dry yeast

1 1/2 cups (375 mL) warm water

1 tsp (5 mL) sugar

2 tsp (10 mL) salt

1 Tbsp (15 mL) vegetable oil

1/4 cup (60 mL) honey

1 large egg

1 egg yolk

4 1/2 cups (1.1 L) all-purpose flour

1 cup (250 mL) poppy seeds

1 Tbsp (15 mL) baking soda

1/3 cup (75 mL) honey

Stir yeast into warm water in a large bowl. Cover bowl with a tea towel and let stand for 5 to 7 minutes, until bubbly. Stir in sugar, salt, oil, first amount of honey, egg and yolk. Add 1 cup (250 mL) flour and stir until combined. Add remaining flour and stir until a dough forms.

Place dough on a floured surface and knead for about 10 minutes, adding flour as necessary, until dough is smooth. Cover with a bowl and let stand for 35 minutes.

Pour poppy seeds into a shallow dish. Set aside. Divide dough into 12 equal portions and roll into rings. Set aside to rise for 15 to 30 minutes. Heat water in a large pot until boiling. Add baking soda and remaining honey and reduce heat to a simmer. Cook bagels, 2 at a time, for 1 minute per side. Remove with a slotted spoon and dip one side into poppy seeds. Place on a baking sheet. Bake in 500°F (260°C) oven until they begin to brown on bottom, about 10 to 12 minutes. Turn bagels over and bake for another 5 to 8 minutes, until golden brown.

Another infamous rivalry is that of the Montréal
bagel versus its New York counterpart. Traditional
Montréal bagels are made with malt, honey and
egg but no salt. They are hand-rolled and boiled in
honey water before being baked in wood-fired
ovens. They differ from New York bagels in that
they are smaller, sweeter and have crispier crust
(and Montréal bagel aficionados would say, are
much better).

Cranberry Chutney

Makes 4 cups (1 L)

The word "cranberry" comes from *craneberry*—the flower looks like the head of a crane, and cranes were known to enjoy the berries. For Canada's First Nations, cranberries were a symbol of peace and were used for food, medicine and even as dyes for textiles. Cranberries were a vital food to both Natives and pioneers because of their naturally occurring benzoic acid, which is a great natural preservative, and their high vitamin C content. Although cranberries are thought of primarily as a Thanksgiving accompaniment, cranberry juice ranks third in sales in North America, after apple and orange. Wild cranberries grow from coast to coast, but a large percentage of Canada's commercial cranberry crop is grown in southwestern B.C.—it is the province's most economically important berry—and the world's largest single-site cranberry farm is situated about 100 kilometres east of Montréal, with other important growing areas in Ontario and the Maritimes. Every fall, cranberry festivals are held in Bala, Ontario, and Fort Langley, B.C.

1 Tbsp (15 mL) unsalted butter

8 oz (250 g) pearl onions or cipollini (small, flattened Italian variety), peeled and left whole

2 Tbsp (30 mL) grated fresh ginger

1 serrano chili, minced

2 kaffir lime leaves or 1 Tbsp (15 mL) lime zest

2 1/4 cups (560 mL) apple cider vinegar

1 cup (250 mL) light brown sugar

1 cup (250 mL) muscovado sugar

2 lbs (1 kg) fresh cranberries

3/4 cup (175 mL) dried fruit such as currants, cranberries, blueberries or sour cherries

sea salt and freshly ground pepper

In a medium-sized pot, melt butter and sauté onions over medium heat for 5 minutes. Add next 6 ingredients and bring to a boil. Add cranberries and dried fruit, turn heat to medium-low and simmer for about 15 minutes or until chutney is thick and has reduced.

Season with salt and pepper, and refrigerate until well chilled.

Tip

Instead of cranberries in this recipe, you could use mango, rhubarb, apple, pear or peach—or experiment using a variety of fruits.

Rhubarb Compote

Makes about 4 cups (1 L)

Indigenous to Asia, rhubarb was brought to Europe by Marco Polo. Plantings have been recorded in Italy since as early as 1608. Huge plantations, mainly for medicinal purposes, were soon established in Oxfordshire and Bedfordshire, England, where they still exist today. Officially recognized in Europe as a food by the 17th century, rhubarb was for a time known as "pie plant" because it was most often presented as a pie filling and in other desserts. The first rhubarb in Canada was brought to Québec by the English. For Canadian pioneers, the robust and hardy rhubarb plant supplied essential vitamins and minerals in spring, before any berries ripened. Patches of rhubarb can still be found dotting the Canadian landscape where no trace of a farmhouse remains. A member of the buckwheat family, rhubarb is closely related to sorrel. Although technically a vegetable, it is used as a fruit in most recipes. Rhubarb compote makes a light dessert on its own or can be used as a sauce for custard and ice cream.

1 cup (250 mL) honey

1/2 cup (125 mL) red wine

1/2 cup (125 mL) unsweetened juice, such as grape or apple

2 sticks cinnamon

1 Tbsp (15 mL) grated fresh ginger

zest of 1 orange

1/2 tsp (2 mL) cardamom

5 cups (1.25 L) chopped fresh rhubarb

3/4 cup (175 mL) dried currants or dried fruit of your choice

Combine first 7 ingredients in a large saucepan over medium heat. Add rhubarb and currants and bring to a boil. Reduce heat and simmer until rhubarb is tender, about 8 minutes. Let cool to room temperature, then cover and refrigerate. Bring to room temperature before serving. Serve compote along with vanilla ice cream, as a topping for toast or as a sauce for cake.

Tip
You can make this recipe into a savoury compote that pairs well with roast pork and game meats. Simply omit the fruit juice, replacing it with 1/3 cup (75 mL) of red wine vinegar, and add 1 finely diced medium red onion with the rhubarb and currants. Continue as per recipe.

Saskatoon Pie

Serves 6

As recently as June 2004, Britain pulled saskatoon products off the shelves, questioning their safety because there was no history of people eating the berries in Europe. Even to many eastern Canadians, the saskatoon (*Amelanchier alnifolia,* also called serviceberry and juneberry) remains a mystery. Interior B.C. and Plains Natives, however, have been enjoying these berries for centuries in everything from pemmican to porridge and, of course, freshly picked. The name "saskatoon" is believed to be a shortened form of the Cree or Blackfoot name for this berry. People who grew up on the Prairies have fond memories of weekend trips to secret saskatoon patches and bountiful harvests that lasted all winter long. The saskatoon, which is related to cherries and apples, has also been an essential winter food for wildlife. Although most prolific on the Prairies, the saskatoon grows from coast to coast and is a truly Canadian berry.

pastry, enough for a double crust (see opposite, or use purchased)

1 egg white, beaten, for brushing crust

6 cups (1.5 L) fresh saskatoons

1/4 cup (60 mL) cornstarch

1 cup (250 mL) unbleached sugar

juice of 1/3 lemon

pinch of sea salt

1 Tbsp (15 mL) unsalted butter

2 Tbsp (30 mL) heavy cream (32%), for brushing

1/4 cup (60 mL) unbleached sugar, for top of crust

Preheat oven to 400° F (200° C). Prepare pastry and line a pie plate. Brush inside of bottom crust with egg white to prevent juices from soaking it and making it soggy. Pick over saskatoons and toss together in a large bowl with cornstarch, sugar, lemon juice and salt. Pour into crust and dot with butter. Secure top crust, being sure to cut air vents. Brush with cream and sprinkle with unbleached sugar. Bake for 12 minutes. Turn heat down to 365° F (185° C) and bake 20 to 30 minutes or until crust is golden brown and filling is bubbly. Place on a wire rack to cool for at least 1 hour.

Tip

For individual free-form pies, as shown below, simply divide pastry into 6 equal portions, roll out to 1/8 inch (3 mm) thick and lay out on a baking sheet lined with parchment paper. Brush with egg white and divide filling evenly amongst rounds, leaving a 1-inch (2.5 cm) border. Fold border up over filling, leaving centre open. Dot with butter, brush with cream and sprinkle with unbleached sugar. Follow baking instructions as above, reducing baking time to about 15 minutes.

Great Pie Crust

2 1/2 cups (625 mL) flour

1 tsp (5 mL) sea salt

1 Tbsp (15 mL) sugar

1 cup (250 mL) unsalted butter, frozen

1 Tbsp (15 mL) lemon juice

about 1/3 cup (75 mL) ice water

Great Pie Crust

Mix flour, salt and sugar in a bowl. Using your cheese grater, grate frozen butter into flour mixture. Toss lightly to distribute butter and add lemon juice and enough water for dough just to come together. Divide in half, wrap each piece in plastic wrap and flatten into a disc. Chill for at least 30 minutes before using. Makes enough for a double-crusted pie.

Shoofly Pie

Serves 6 to 8

This tasty pie of Swiss or Pennsylvania Dutch Mennonite origin gets its name from the inevitable need to shoo flies away from its sugary filling as it cools on the windowsill, yet—surprisingly—it is not overly sweet. The ingredients were staples that could stave off hunger when perishables were unavailable. Seeking freedom to practise their beliefs and lifestyle, and unsure of their future after the American Revolution, Swiss Mennonites first came to Canada from Pennsylvania in 1786. Small groups of Amish Mennonites followed throughout the 19th century. From the 1870s through to the end of World War II, several waves of Mennonites came from Russia and Germany, also seeking farmland and freedom. Ontario and Manitoba were popular destinations, but some Mennonites chose Saskatchewan, Alberta or southwestern B.C. Because the Mennonites were farmers and generally chose to live separate from the rest of society, their culinary tradition is strong, bringing influences from many cuisines and many generations. Today, Winnipeg has one of the world's largest urban Mennonite populations.

pastry, enough for a single crust (see p. 125, or use purchased)

1 tsp (5 mL) baking soda

3/4 cup (175 mL) molasses

1 cup (250 mL) boiling water

pinch of sea salt

pinch of ginger

1 1/2 cups (375 mL) flour

1 cup (250 mL) dark brown sugar

3/4 cup (175 mL) butter

1/2 tsp (2 mL) cinnamon

Preheat oven to 375° F (190° C). Line pie plate with pastry. In a bowl, stir soda into molasses until foamy, then add water, salt and ginger and set aside.

Mix flour with brown sugar and cut in butter. Add cinnamon and stir until crumbly. Pour 1/3 of molasses mixture into pie, sprinkle with 1/3 of crumble and continue to layer, ending with crumble on top. Bake for 35 to 40 minutes.

Tip
Shoofly pie will keep for up to 5 days in an airtight container. For a variation on this recipe, add 1 cup (250 mL) chopped dried fruit to crumble mixture.

Pies have been part of traditional cuisine at least as far back as the Ancient Greeks, and many cultures have their own variations of savoury or sweet pies. Pies have a place in popular culture as well; old-time comedy acts often contained a pie thrower and a victim. In the political arena, recipients of a cream pie in the face at the hands of dissatisfied constituents have included prime ministers Jean Chrétien and Joe Clark and premiers Ralph Klein (Alberta) and Bill Vander Zalm (B.C.).

Québec Sugar Pie

Serves 8

This very sweet yet irresistible treat is synonymous with French Canadian cooking and the arrival of spring—it would not be maple syrup harvest time without sugar pie. This dish, which is called *tarte au sucre* in French, may have originated from the endless honey cakes and desserts found throughout France. Because maple syrup was so abundant and easy to harvest in the Maritimes, Acadians would have used it or maple sugar in many dishes instead of the traditional honey or imported sugar or molasses. Every Québec family seems to have its own favourite version of this pie, but brown sugar and heavy cream are usually key ingredients. This recipe is an adaptation of traditional Acadian sugar pie. A similar and equally popular dessert, "gâteau de sirop" in the Cajun cuisine of the American South, was also a gift from our Acadian ancestors.

1 1/2 cups (375 mL) brown sugar

1/2 cup (125 mL) maple sugar

2 Tbsp (30 mL) flour

1 cup (250 mL) heavy cream (32%)

1 tsp (5 mL) pure vanilla extract

pinch of nutmeg (optional)

pinch of sea salt

1/2 cup (125 mL) chopped nuts such as pecans or walnuts (optional)

pastry, enough for a single crust (see p. 125, or use purchased)

Preheat oven to 350° F (175° C). Bring sugars, flour and cream to a boil over low heat and simmer for about 10 minutes or until thickened. Stir in vanilla, nutmeg, salt and nuts, if using. Pour into a prepared pie crust and bake for 30 to 35 minutes.

Allow to cool to room temperature before serving. Serve with fresh fruit and lightly whipped cream.

Tip
This pie will keep for up to 5 days in an airtight container.

There are many versions of sugar pie in Québec. In Gaspé, oats are added to the pie, and evaporated milk is used instead of cream. In the Laurentians, maple syrup is not as plentiful, and sugar pie is generally made simply with brown sugar. In Acadian kitchens, the pie is enriched with whole eggs.

Rum 'n' Pumpkin Pie

Serves at least 8

Pumpkins and other squashes are New World plants (*Cucurbita* genus) that humans have cultivated as food crops for at least 7000 years. Through trade, species originating in Mexico and Central America spread northward to Canada, becoming important crops for many First Nations; the flesh was consumed raw or roasted, the flowers and seeds were sometimes eaten and the skins could be cut into strips, dried and made into mats. In the 17th century, the English name for this squash was "pompion," which eventually became "pumpkin." British immigrants soon discovered that pumpkins were much easier for carving jack-o'-lanterns than the turnips or potatoes used back in Ireland and Scotland or the beets used in England. As one of many ways of using pumpkins, colonists filled whole ones with milk and spices and then baked them in fire pits; transferred to a pastry crust, these ingredients became pumpkin pie as we know it today.

pastry, enough for a single crust (see p. 125, or use purchased)

1 egg, beaten, for egg wash

2 cups (500 mL) pumpkin purée (see Tip)

1/2 cup (125 mL) corn syrup

2/3 cup (150 mL) brown sugar

2 eggs, lightly beaten, for filling

1 cup (250 mL) heavy cream (32%)

1/4 cup (60 mL) dark rum

1 tsp (5 mL) pure vanilla extract

1/2 tsp (2 mL) each cinnamon and ginger

1/4 tsp (1 mL) each nutmeg and sea salt

whipped cream (32%) for garnish

Preheat oven to 375° F (190° C). Line pie plate(s) with pastry, brush with egg wash and chill.

In a bowl, whisk together remaining ingredients, except whipped cream, until smooth and uniform. Pour filling into prepared shell and bake for about 50 minutes or until filling is set—the slightly wobbly centre will continue to set as it cools.

My friend Ruth, a very talented pastry chef, makes her pumpkin pie by using 1 cup (250 mL) coconut milk instead of cream. It adds an amazing flavour and is worth trying, especially if you or any of your guests are lactose intolerant.

Allow pie to cool completely at room temperature before serving with whipped cream. This recipe makes one 6-cup (1.5 L) or two 3-cup (750 mL) pies.

Tip
Make your own pumpkin purée, or buy canned pumpkin purée; avoid canned pie filling, which already has a variety of spices added to it.

Coconut-scented Butter Tarts

Makes 12 butter tarts

Butter tarts mean as much—or more—to Canadians as Yorkshire pudding to the English, croissants to the French or haggis to the Scots, and they are just as much of a national symbol. Canadian butter tarts may have developed from the gooey, delicate, crusted treat called the Ecclefechan butter tart. This tart, named after the town of Ecclefechan, Scotland, was brought to Canada by Scottish immigrants who reached Pictou, Nova Scotia, on September 15, 1773. Some people believe butter tarts are related to Québec's sugar pie, and there is no denying their similarity to southern Creole pecan pie. Whatever the origin, the recipe first appeared in a Canadian cookbook *(Five Roses Cookbook)* in 1915. Because of its common ingredients and simple procedure, it has endured in our hearts and recipe books. I consider coconut to be an improvement in most recipes, and butter tarts are no exception. For an authentic butter tart recipe, use raisins or currants instead of the coconut, or omit them both for an "au naturel" version.

pastry, enough for a double crust (see p. 125, or use purchased pastry)	Preheat oven to 425° F (220° C). Lightly butter 12-muffin tin and line cups with pastry. Sprinkle coconut evenly into crusts.
1 cup (250 mL) unsweetened coconut, toasted (see Tip)	In a bowl, beat eggs. Add remaining ingredients and stir gently just to combine; overstirring filling can make it bubble over during baking. Pour egg mixture over coconut to fill muffin cups 3/4 full. Bake until just set, about 15 minutes. Serve at room temperature, garnished with chocolate shavings and fresh berries.
2 eggs	
1 cup (250 mL) brown sugar	
1 cup (250 mL) corn syrup	
1/2 cup (125 mL) unsalted butter	**Tip**
1 1/2 tsp (7 mL) pure vanilla extract	To toast coconut, preheat oven to 350° F (175° C), place coconut on a baking sheet and bake for 3 to 5 minutes, stirring often and watching carefully so it doesn't burn.
1 tsp (5 mL) cider vinegar	
1/4 tsp (1 mL) sea salt	The tarts will keep for 1 week in a sealed container and up to 1 month if frozen.

For optimal freshness, store nuts, such as coconut and almonds, in the freezer, because they can go rancid quickly at room temperature. If there is room, keep flours and foods with a high oil content, such as poppy seeds, in the freezer as well.

Doughnuts

Makes 18 doughnuts

Every civilization has munched sweetened, deep-fried dough in one form or another, including Dutch *olykoeks* or *oliebollen*, but doughnuts as we know them today—round with a hole in the centre—originated in New England. Canadians have made them their own, though. We have more doughnut shops and eat more doughnuts per capita than any other country, thanks largely to the Tim Hortons franchise, founded in 1964 in Hamilton by NHL defenceman Tim Horton. With this recipe, try frying up the doughnut holes, too, to make your own "Timbits."

1 1/2 Tbsp (22 mL) butter

1 1/2 tsp (7 mL) salt

1 tsp (5 mL) ground nutmeg

1/4 cup (60 mL) sugar

3/4 cup (175 mL) milk, scalded

1 large egg, beaten

1 tsp (5 mL) sugar

1/4 cup (60 mL) warm water

1 envelope (1 Tbsp [15 mL]) active dry yeast

3 1/4 cups (800 mL) all-purpose flour

3 cups (750 mL) cooking oil

1 cup (250 mL) sugar

Combine butter, salt, nutmeg and first amount of sugar in a large bowl. Stir in scalded milk. Cool to lukewarm.

Mix in beaten egg.

Stir remaining sugar in warm water in a small bowl. Sprinkle yeast over top. Let stand 10 minutes. Stir to dissolve yeast. Add to batter.

Work in enough flour until dough pulls away from sides of bowl. Turn out onto a floured surface. Knead 8 to 10 minutes until smooth and elastic. Place in a greased bowl, turning once to grease top. Cover with a tea towel. Let stand in oven with light on and door closed for about 1 1/2 hours until doubled in size. Punch dough down. Cover with a tea towel. Let stand in oven with light on and door closed for 30 minutes. Roll out 1/2 inch (12 mm) thick on lightly floured board. Cut with a doughnut cutter. Place doughnuts on baking sheet. Cover with a tea towel. Let stand in oven with light on and door closed for about 1 hour until doubled in size.

Deep-fry in hot 375°F (190°C) oil, placing raised side (top side) down until brown. Turn to brown other side. Drain on paper towels.

Sprinkle with sugar while hot, if desired.

Beaver tails (also known as elephant ears) are a uniquely Canadian doughnut cousin. Once a baked, waste-not, want-not delicacy enjoyed by First Nations, the words have evolved to mean a fried slab of risen dough dusted with cinnamon and sugar or any number of toppings. Trademarked by Pam and Grant Hooker and first served at Ottawa's ByWard Market, beaver tails are a treat today enjoyed nationwide.

Pets de Soeur

Makes 24 pastries

It was Samuel de Champlain who brought the Roman Catholic Church to New France. The French clergy and aristocracy supported the establishment of various orders, including the Jesuits, to create schools and hospitals in the St. Lawrence Valley and beyond. In the early days of the French Canadian *habitants,* the Catholic Church formed the backbone of the community, providing structure and support; the church was also a strong, overbearing and often-feared influence. This situation created somewhat of a love-hate relationship between the Church and the parishioners, and many derogatory phrases sprang from this time. Thankfully, these little cinnamon pastries taste nothing like their name; *pets de soeur* literally translates as "nun's farts."

Dough

3 cups (750 mL) all-purpose flour

2 tsp (10 mL) baking powder

1 tsp (5 mL) sea salt

1/2 cup (125 mL) chilled butter

1 cup (250 mL) milk

Filling

1/4 cup (60 mL) butter, softened

1 cup (250 mL) brown sugar

1 tsp (5 mL) ground cinnamon

Preheat oven to 375° F (190° C). Line a baking sheet with parchment paper. Sift dry dough ingredients together. Using a fork, cut butter into dry ingredients until it resembles coarse meal. Add milk to form a dough. Cover and let rest for 15 minutes.

Roll dough out as thin as you would for a pie crust. Butter dough and sprinkle evenly with brown sugar and cinnamon. Roll dough up like a jelly roll and cut into 1/4-inch (6 mm) slices. Bake for 15 to 20 minutes or until golden brown.

Tip

Pets de soeur make a great gift. They will keep for up to 2 weeks in a sealed container.

The French were not the only nationality to draw from the Catholic Church when naming sweet treats. The famous Portuguese desserts barrigas de freira *(nun's tummies)* and papos de anjo *(angel cheeks) were created and perfected by nuns during the 17th and 18th centuries.*

Maple Sugar Cookies

Makes about 4 dozen 3-inch (7.5 cm) cookies

Québec's early French settlers were introduced to maple syrup by local First Nations peoples, who collected the sap in hollowed-out logs. The syrup quickly became an invaluable part of the *habitant* diet. It is said that, until the 1950s, the average family of Québec's Beauce region consumed about 100 kilograms of maple products per year. Québec provides about 90% of Canada's and 75% of the world's maple syrup, a quarter of which comes from the Beauce area. It takes roughly the amount of sap drawn from a typical tree each season—about 40 litres—to make one litre of syrup, and the region now produces about 9 million litres of syrup annually. Commercial maple syrup comes mostly from the sugar maple (*Acer saccharum*) and the black maple (*A. nigrum*). Other types of maples are also tapped, but their saps are less plentiful with a lower sugar content and are not as favoured. More than a sweetener, maple syrup also contains several important minerals.

2 cups (500 mL) all-purpose, unbleached flour

1 tsp (5 mL) baking powder

pinch of sea salt

1 cup (250 mL) unsalted butter, at room temperature

1 cup (250 mL) maple sugar, plus additional for dusting

1/2 cup (125 mL) brown sugar

1 tsp (5 mL) pure vanilla extract

1 egg

1 Tbsp (15 mL) maple syrup, plus additional for brushing

Preheat oven to 350° F (175° C). Sift together flour, baking powder and salt. Cream together butter and sugars. Add vanilla. Beat in egg and maple syrup. Fold in flour mixture, and stir to form a dough, being sure not to over mix. Roll dough out 1/8 inch (3 mm) thick on a lightly floured surface. Cut with cookie cutter, and place cookies on a parchment-lined baking sheet.

Brush tops of cookies with maple syrup and sprinkle with maple sugar. Bake for 5 to 8 minutes or until edges just start to colour.

Tip
The dough can be formed into a disc, tightly wrapped and refrigerated for up to 3 days. The dough can also be frozen for up to 1 month. Allow it to come to room temperature before using.

The word "cookie" comes from the Dutch word koekje, meaning "little cake." Cookies had a humble beginning as test cakes—a little cake batter was put into the oven to ensure the proper temperature—but these little cakes soon began to command their own audience, and they proved to be an ideal travelling food.

Nanaimo Bars

Makes 12 squares

Nanaimo is a picturesque community on Vancouver Island. The Nanaimo District Museum receives so many inquiries into the origins of the Nanaimo bar that it is considering developing an exhibit in honour of this treat. There are at least three similar bar recipes from the early 1950s. One, called "chocolate slice," appeared in *The Women's Auxiliary to the Nanaimo Hospital Cook Book* (1952); a second, published in the *Vancouver Sun,* was called "Nanaimo bars"; and a third, called "Mrs. Gayton's Bars," was printed in a 1955 cookbook put out by St. Aidan's United Church in Victoria. Around this time, the test kitchens of several food companies also developed various Nanaimo bar recipes to promote use of their products. Whatever its origin, the Nanaimo bar is a tasty treat.

Layer 1

1/2 cup (125 mL) butter

1/4 cup (60 mL) sugar

2 Tbsp (30 mL) cocoa

1 egg

2 cups (500 mL) graham cracker crumbs

1 cup (250 mL) shredded coconut

1/2 cup (125 mL) toasted, chopped nuts of your choice

1 tsp (5 mL) pure vanilla extract

Layer 2

1/4 cup (60 mL) half and half cream (10–18%)

2 Tbsp (30 mL) custard powder

3 Tbsp (45 mL) butter

1 tsp (5 mL) pure vanilla extract

2 cups (500 mL) sifted icing sugar

Layer 3

5 oz (140 g) semi-sweet chocolate

2 Tbsp (30 mL) butter

Layer 1
Soften butter in a double boiler. Add sugar, cocoa and egg and then heat until slightly thickened. Stir in rest of ingredients, and press mixture into a 9-inch (23 cm) square pan. Chill 15 minutes.

Layer 2
Mix ingredients together and spread evenly over first layer. Chill 15 minutes.

Layer 3
Melt chocolate and butter together until smooth and spread over second layer. Chill 15 minutes. Score top with a sharp knife to make 12 squares, then cut and serve or store in an airtight container for up to 1 week.

Espresso Nanimo Bars
Add 2 tsp (10 mL) instant espresso powder and 2 Tbsp (30 mL) heavy cream (32%) to second layer. Once third layer has been spread, stud centre of each square with a chocolate-covered coffee bean. Chill, cut and serve.

Pistachio Ginger Nanaimo Bars
(featured in photo) Use 1/2 cup (125 mL) chopped unsalted pistachios as nuts in first layer. When third layer has been spread, sprinkle 1 cup (250 mL) of finely diced candied ginger over it. Chill, cut and serve.

Fig and Date Matrimonial Cake

Makes 12 to 16 squares

"Matrimonial cake" is a uniquely western-Canadian name for the popular treat that is better known as date squares. Some people believe the dessert may have come by the unusual name through its association with the "shivaree" or "chiverie." Scarcely practised today, this old custom involved a midnight visit to rouse unsuspecting newlyweds by shouting, shooting guns and clanging pots and pans. Often, the entire town participated, usually fortified by liquid encouragement. Afterward, there would be visiting, dancing, games and refreshments prepared by the neighbouring women, matrimonial cake being a standard offering. The tradition originated in France (as le *charivari*) and was most likely passed on through the Acadians. In this recipe, the cane sugar commonly used in the crust has been substituted with date sugar, which is simply ground-up dried dates and is available in large grocery stores and health food stores.

1 cup (250 mL) chopped dates

2 cups (500 mL) chopped dried figs

1 cup (250 mL) water

1 1/2 cups (375 mL) whole-wheat flour

1 tsp (5 mL) baking powder

1/2 tsp (2 mL) baking soda

1 cup (250 mL) butter

1 1/2 cups (375 mL) rolled oats

1 cup (250 mL) date sugar (or brown sugar)

Cook dates and figs in water to make a soft, spreadable mixture, about 10 minutes; let cool.

Preheat oven to 350° F (175° C). Blend dry ingredients, except oats and sugar, and cut butter in with a fork. Add oats and sugar. Press half of this mixture into an 8-inch (20 cm) square pan. Spread with date and fig filling, top with remaining oat mixture and bake for 25 to 30 minutes.

Tip
These bars can stored for up to 1 week in an airtight container.

With fruit sometimes known as nature's candy, the date palm could be the tree with the longest history of cultivation, perhaps dating back to 6000 BC. Every part of the date palm may be eaten, from the leaves to the roots, and even the seeds can be ground and used with flour to make bread. This "Tree of Life," a holy symbol for Muslims, is thought to be native to the shores of the Persian Gulf. The date palm has been grown in California since the 1890s; the industry there now produces nearly 30,000 metric tonnes of dates a year, which may seem like a lot, but countries such as Iraq and Saudi Arabia have harvests 15 times as large.

Blueberry Crisp

Serves 4 to 6

Blueberries, which grow across much of the country, were a significant food source for Canada's Indigenous peoples, and parts of the plant were also important in medical uses. A favourite Inuit preparation of blueberries is to preserve them in fish oil. About half of Canada's commercial blueberry harvest comes from cultivated highbush varieties *(Vaccinium corymbosum),* with the rest supplied by managed stands of wild lowbush berries *(V. angustifolium* and *V. myrtilloides).* Southwestern B.C. produces most of Canada's cultivated berries. "Wild blues" are smaller, with a deeper blue colour and more intense blueberry flavour than the cultivated berries. Oxford, Nova Scotia, the "blueberry capital of the world," has the perfect climate for growing lowbush blueberries. With contributions from other Atlantic provinces and Québec, Canada is the world's largest supplier of lowbush blueberries. Bursting with flavour, full of antioxidants and containing very few calories, blueberries are said to be among the healthiest of foods.

Base

4 cups (1 L) fresh or frozen blueberries

1/4 cup (60 mL) sugar or honey

juice and zest of 1/2 lemon

1/4 cup (60 mL) chopped fresh basil or mint

2 Tbsp (30 mL) flour

Topping

1/2 cup (125 mL) brown sugar

1/2 cup (125 mL) rolled oats

1/2 cup (125 mL) flour

1/3 cup (75 mL) softened unsalted butter

1 tsp (5 mL) cinnamon

Preheat oven to 375° F (190° C). Combine base ingredients and pour into a buttered 6-cup (1.5 L) baking dish.

Combine topping ingredients in a bowl until uniform and sprinkle over berry base. Bake for 25 to 30 minutes. Serve warm or at room temperature with ice cream or whipped cream.

Tip
Crisps are very versatile and can be made with almost any fruit or combination of fruits—try apples, rhubarb or peaches.

Select fresh blueberries that are firm and have a lively, uniform colour; avoid dull, soft or watery berries. Blueberries can be stored in the refrigerator for up to a week, but they are best used within a couple of days of purchase. You can also freeze them for later use.

Blueberry Grunt

Serves 6

Sometimes called a "slump," this traditional Maritime dessert proves that summer evenings in Canada can be cool enough to enjoy a hot dessert. This dish, which "grunts" as it cooks away, probably came to Canada by way of the more than 30,000 New England Loyalists who settled here during the American Revolution. Historically, dumplings were Northern Europe's answer to the pasta dishes of the South. The Mi'kmaq-favoured blueberry became a natural match for dumplings, although you can find grunts made with huckleberries or rhubarb. It has been speculated that, with the widespread availability of ovens, the cobbler and the pandowdy (dowdy) became popular baked variations using similar ingredients. The difference is that a cobbler has the dough as a crust on top of (or surrounding) the fruit, and with a pandowdy, the dough is cut into squares and layered in a patchwork pattern over the fruit, allowing some syrup to bubble over the pastry while baking.

4 to 5 cups (1 to 1.25 L) fresh blueberries

1 cup (250 mL) sugar

1 cup (250 mL) blueberry juice (available bottled in grocery and health food stores—or reconstitute unsweetened frozen concentrate)

1 1/2 cups (375 mL) flour

2 tsp (10 mL) baking powder

2 Tbsp (30 mL) grated lime zest

1/2 tsp (2 mL) cinnamon

1/8 tsp (0.5 mL) freshly ground nutmeg

1/4 tsp (1 mL) sea salt

1/2 cup (125 mL) unsalted butter, frozen

1 cup (250 mL) milk

In a wide saucepan, combine blueberries, sugar and juice to make a sauce. Bring to a boil, reduce heat and simmer for 10 minutes.

Sift flour and baking powder into a bowl and add lime zest, cinnamon, nutmeg and salt. With a cheese grater, grate frozen butter into flour mixture and toss. Pour in milk and mix lightly to form a dough for dumplings. Let dough rest, refrigerated, for 1 hour.

Drop dumplings, 1 tablespoon at a time, into hot blueberry sauce. Cover and cook for about 15 minutes or until dumplings are cooked. Serve hot, spooning some dumplings and sauce into each bowl, and top with whipped cream or crème fraîche (see opposite).

Tip
Allow enough time to freeze the butter and for the dough to rest.

Crème Fraîche

You can buy crème fraîche or make your own.

Combine cream and buttermilk. Leave on countertop for 24 hours, then cover and refrigerate up to 10 days.

Crème Fraîche

1 cup (250 mL) heavy cream (32%)

2 Tbsp (30 mL) buttermilk

Grand Pères

A French Canadian twist! Omit blueberries, sugar and blueberry juice from blueberry grunt recipe and continue with dumpling portion. After dough has rested, bring 4 cups (1 L) maple syrup to a boil and drop dough by tablespoon into hot syrup, cover pot and cook for 15 minutes. To serve, spoon some dumplings and syrup into each bowl and sprinkle with icing sugar.

Pulled Molasses Taffy

Makes 24 to 30 pieces

The word "taffy" means "beloved" in Welsh. The *Oxford English Dictionary* dates the first use of the word to 1825, although the making of taffy undoubtedly goes back much further. Taffy's origin in Canada is attributed to St. Marguerite Bourgeoys, who came to Canada from France in 1653. She was the founder of the Sisters of the Congregation of Notre-Dame, the first community of religious women in the New World, and was responsible for building the first stone chapel in Montréal. Pulled taffy and the history of St. Marguerite have remained a strong tradition throughout French Canada. For young children, taffy pulling is a popular school activity on November 25—the feast day of St. Catherine, patron saint of unmarried girls—and on January 12—St. Marguerite's feast day.

2 cups (500 mL) brown sugar

2 cups (500 mL) unsulphured molasses

2 Tbsp (30 mL) vinegar

1/2 cup (125 mL) water

1/2 tsp (2 mL) baking soda

1 Tbsp (15 mL) butter

pinch of sea salt

Butter a jelly roll pan thoroughly. Bring brown sugar, molasses, vinegar and water to a boil in a heavy-bottomed pan without stirring. Continue to boil until it reaches 260° F (130° C) .

Stir in baking soda, butter and salt. Pour into prepared pan and, using a spatula, fold onto itself until cool enough to handle.

With buttered hands, gather taffy and stretch until it is a light caramel colour and is no longer easily pliable. Twist into a rope, cut into pieces (buttered scissors work best) and wrap in wax paper or decorative candy paper (available in craft stores).

Tip
Molasses taffy will stay fresh, wrapped and kept in a sealed container, for up to 2 weeks.

Molasses (treacle) is a thick syrup made from sugar cane, sugar beets or sorghum. The colour and consistency depend on the type and degree of processing. Unsulphured molasses is a high-quality, light-coloured, delicately flavoured syrup. The production of sulphured molasses, which is heavier and sweeter, involves treating unripe sugar cane with sulphur fumes. Blackstrap molasses is a dark, thick, less-sweet byproduct of sugar production that is chosen for its distinctive flavour and higher mineral content. Using molasses will acquaint you with the meaning of someone being "as slow as molasses in January."

McIntosh Apple Ice

Serves 6

In 1811, John McIntosh (1777–1845) discovered about 20 apple trees growing in a wooded area of his farm, near what is now Prescott, Ontario. He transplanted some of them, and one of the transplants produced a fruit he considered superior. His son Allen was instrumental in the apple's spread, through teaching many surrounding farmers how to reproduce the delicious fruit tree using grafting and budding techniques. The original McIntosh apple tree lived for over 90 years and was left standing to commemorate the hard work and dedication of the McIntosh family. Apples are Canada's largest fruit crop, and the McIntosh—the only variety grown in all apple-growing regions of Canada—makes up half of all Canadian apple production. Macs are excellent raw or in pies, cakes, crisps, butters and ciders—one a day to keep the doctor away!

1 cup (250 mL) apple juice or water

5 cups (1.25 L) McIntosh apple slices, cored

1 cup (250 mL) honey

1 tsp (5 mL) lime zest

3 Tbsp (45 mL) tequila

Bring juice, apples, honey and zest to a boil. Reduce heat and simmer for 5 to 7 minutes or until apples are tender. Pour into a processor fitted with blade attachment and purée, adding tequila. Pour purée into a shallow baking dish and freeze until firm, about 3 hours. Return mixture to processor and pulse until chunks are chipped and fluffy. Store frozen in an airtight container for up to 5 days. Re-pulse before serving if ice becomes too hard.

Bumbleberry Pie

If you wander into a country café and order a wedge of bumbleberry pie, you will be digging into a double-crusted, Merlot-coloured delight. You may wonder, is the bumbleberry an object of desire for the bumblebee? Is it one of the over 2000 varieties of blackberry? Made with a mixture of berries—chef's choice, of course—but often a blend of raspberries, blueberries and blackberries, bumbleberry pie is usually enriched with apples and often rhubarb.

Iced Tea with Fresh Mint

Serves 4

Tea, in its many variations, is a beverage enjoyed worldwide. Across Canada, tea-rooms serve a variety of teas, both iced and hot. Although every type of tea imaginable can be found in multicultural Canada today, one brand in particular is known as Canada's brand: Red Rose. In 1894, Theodore Harding Estabrooks opened his business in Saint John, New Brunswick, blending and packing high-quality teas. Red Rose tea quickly expanded throughout Atlantic Canada and eventually the rest of the country. Iced tea can be made with any tea you like, from the standard black tea to green tea and even herbal teas, but some would say that Red Rose's orange pekoe makes one of the best.

6 cups (1.5 L) cold water

5 tsp (25 mL) good quality, loose tea

2/3 cup (150 mL) sugar, or to taste

1 handful of fresh mint, rinsed and patted dry

1 lime or lemon

Bring 4 cups (1 L) of water to a boil. Place the tea in a pitcher and pour the boiling water over the tea. Let infuse for 30 minutes.

Stir in sugar to dissolve and strain tea into a clean pitcher. Add the remaining water.

Bruise the mint by crushing it lightly with a rolling pin or the bottom of a glass and place in the pitcher.

Chill tea for at least 1 hour. Remove mint before serving, and serve with a wedge of lime or lemon and a sprig of mint, if desired.

Labrador Tea
Serves 4

The Labrador tea plant (Ledum groenlandicum) is a member of the Heath family and is related to blueberries and cranberries. The leaves have been used for centuries by Native peoples in a tea, which is also known as swamp tea or Hudson's Bay tea. Believed to possess medicinal qualities, it was applied topically for skin irritations and rashes and made into syrup for coughs and sore throats. It was also thought to aid in digestion and stimulate the nerves. Labrador tea is high in vitamin C, which was an important addition to the diet of Natives and settlers alike. Labrador tea is still enjoyed throughout the Maritimes and is even available in tea bag form.

To make Labrador tea, steep about 15 leaves in 4 cups (1 L) of boiling water for 8 minutes. Strain and serve, sweetened if desired.

Some people call the alcohol-spiked version of iced tea "iced tea on a stick." Iced coffee is also a popular summer drink available homemade or purchased from fine coffee shops throughout the country.

Bloody Caesar
Serves 1

Now known as Canada's national drink, this concoction was invented by Walter Chell in 1969. As the head bartender at the Calgary Inn (now the Westin), he was asked to come up with a new drink to celebrate the opening of a new Italian restaurant on the premises. Chell experimented for three months to find the right combination and settled on hand-mashed clams, tomato juice, vodka, Worcestershire sauce, salt and pepper, with a celery stick for garnish. To spare bartenders and drinkers the hassle of mashing clams every time a Bloody Caesar was ordered, American entrepreneur Duffy Mott soon developed Clamato juice with Chell's assistance, and now Canadians drink about 310 million Caesars every year. Several kinds of Clamato juice are now available, with different levels of spiciness to suite your palate.

celery salt

1 oz (30 mL) vodka

Clamato juice, as needed

dash of Worcestershire sauce

dash of Tabasco

sea salt and pepper to taste

1 stalk celery

Rim a tall glass with celery salt. Add vodka and fill glass with Clamato juice. Add remaining ingredients and stir. Garnish with celery stalk.

Pepper Vodka
To make your own pepper vodka to use in this recipe, simply toast 1/3 cup (75 mL) whole peppercorns in a dry pot over medium-low heat until their aroma is released, about 2 minutes. Remove from heat, and pour a bottle of good-quality clear vodka into pot. Let infuse for 1 hour, then pour back into bottle, including pepper. Keep in freezer (how all vodka should be stored) and use in your favourite cocktails.

Calgary Red Eye
A mixture very popular in southern Alberta, a Calgary Red Eye is 1 part tomato juice and 2 parts beer.

P'tit Caribou
Serves many!

Early traders would mix the ingredients for this very alcoholic beverage together in an earthenware jug and bury it to age it. The name, "little caribou," is said to come from the red colour that reminded hunters of caribou blood. The recipe below is a traditional version, but one modernized P'tit Caribou calls for red wine, whisky, crème de cassis and—surprise, surprise—maple syrup.

40 oz (1.18 L) white alcohol (vodka is best)

40 oz (1.18L) sherry, port or red wine

Mix together and age for at least 48 hours, refrigerated.

P'tit Caribou   Calgary Red Eye   Bloody Caesar

Blueberry or Blackberry Wine

Makes about 12 bottles

Canada now produces a broad range of wines. Icewine is a sweet, complex nectar of German origin, yet Canada has become the world leader for quality and quantity, winning countless gold medals. Brock University in St. Catharines, Ontario, even boasts a world-class Cool Climate Oenology and Viticulture Institute, producing the first Canadian winemakers to learn their craft on home turf. Canada's success is not confined to icewine. More and more Canadian wines are earning a reputation within the country and abroad. The Niagara Peninsula, for example, is situated at the same latitude as Burgundy, with similar soil and climate, and it has recently attracted the interest of French investors. The following recipes will not produce wines of competition calibre, but they are enjoyable and easy to make at home.

8 cups (2 L) blueberries or blackberries

16 cups (4 L) boiling water

10 cups (2.5 L) granulated sugar

4 cups (1 L) prunes

Put berries into a large container that will not react to acids. Bring water to a boil and pour over berries. Let sit for 2 days, stirring occasionally. Strain.

Stir in sugar. Boil this mixture for 5 minutes, then add prunes. Place in a large crock, cover with cheesecloth and let sit for 2 months. Strain and bottle.

Age bottles at least 6 months before drinking.

Dandelion Wine

Makes about 12 bottles

about 15 cups (3.8 L) water

about 15 cups (3.8 L) dandelion blooms, washed and spun dry

3 lemons, peeled and sliced

3 oranges, peeled and sliced

2 cups (500 mL) unsulphured dried apricots

3 lbs (1.5 kg) granulated sugar

1 cake of brewer's yeast, available from your local home brewing store

Bring water to a boil and pour over dandelion blooms in a large container that resists acids. Let sit for 24 hours.

Strain liquid and stir lemons, oranges, apricots, sugar and yeast. Let sit for 3 to 6 weeks, then strain again and bottle.

Age bottles at least 2 months before drinking.

INDEX